I0984787

The Innovation Navigator

Transforming Your Organization in the Era of Digital Design and Collaborative Culture

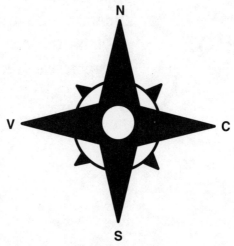

37.797173 | -122.27623
55.676097 | 12.568337
55.861085 | -4.251898

The Innovation Navigator

Transforming Your
Organization in the Era
of Digital Design and
Collaborative Culture

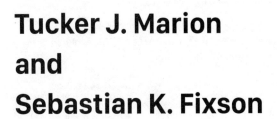

**Tucker J. Marion
and
Sebastian K. Fixson**

UNIVERSITY OF TORONTO PRESS
Toronto Buffalo London

ISBN 978-1-4875-0111-2

∞ Printed on acid-free, 100% post-consumer recycled paper
with vegetable-based inks.

Library and Archives Canada Cataloguing in Publication

Marion, Tucker J., author
The innovation navigator : transforming your organization in the era of
digital design and collaborative culture/Tucker J. Marion and Sebastian
K. Fixson.

Includes bibliographical references and index.
ISBN 978-1-4875-0111-2 (cloth)

1. Organizational change.   2. Technological innovations.   I. Fixson,
Sebastian K., 1967–, author   II. Title.

HD58.8.M267 2018   658.4'06   C2018-903875-6

University of Toronto Press acknowledges the financial assistance to its
publishing program of the Canada Council for the Arts and the Ontario Arts
Council, an agency of the Government of Ontario.

Canada Council   Conseil des Arts
for the Arts   du Canada

ONTARIO ARTS COUNCIL
CONSEIL DES ARTS DE L'ONTARIO
an Ontario government agency
un organisme du gouvernement de l'Ontario

Funded by the   Financé par le
Government   gouvernement
of Canada   du Canada

Canadä

For Kate, Eliza, and Avery

For Stefanie, Hannah, and Leonard

Contents

Foreword

by Ric Fulop
Founder and CEO, Desktop Metal, Inc.

I have spent my career launching new technologies, both as an entrepreneur and as an investor. Many of these technologies were focused on making the design and creation of products easier and faster. An important underlying force that made these new solutions possible is the tremendous advancement of digital technologies. Today, every one of us has more computing power in our pocket via a smartphone than the NASA Apollo mission to the moon could marshal. The ubiquity and low cost of computing power, together with new ways of collaborating, is enabling entirely new ways to innovate.

In this book, the authors discuss how two forces – digital design and a collaborative culture – are moving us from the pre-digital age into the digital era. In this new era, these two forces are paving the way for transformative breakthroughs, not only in the speed with which we can prototype, but in the designs themselves and how they are manufactured. These new opportunities will reshape how firms approach design, development, and manufacturing and how they organize themselves and involve others in the process. Cloud-based CAD (computer-aided design) to facilitate distributed collaboration, design optimization via generative design, real-time engineering analysis, increasingly fast and near-net-shaped custom prototyping and production 3D printing, and exponential growth of collaborative communication platforms like Slack are examples of this trend. The pace is breathtaking. We are living in an exciting time, and the firms that best implement these new technologies and platforms will have a competitive advantage.

At Desktop Metal, we are focusing on all three areas – prototyping, enabling design innovation, and transforming manufacturing. For the design engineer, we offer unique tools to help design and render near-production-strength parts very early in the process. Rapid prototyping for almost three decades was about appearance and form. And while this was extremely important to see the shape of housings or feel the actual size of a device, the usefulness was limited. Plastics have improved, but many of the most important aspects of design and engineering require real material strength. Think of a key structural part of an automobile suspension link or a new propeller design for a boat. Now we can design, have instant checks of critical design elements, and test in the real world in a matter of hours, sometimes even less. And this will only improve. Within five years the cycle time will drop dramatically, as will the cost per unit volume of material. On the manufacturing side, many words are written about the promise of additive manufacturing: desktop factories in every home. While that may be possible one day, we are focused on transforming the factory floor today. Today's manufacturing facilities need to be agile, to reduce changeover time, and to respond to changes in demand and model type. Industrial additive manufacturing can do this, and it has the ability to decentralize the manufacturing process. In this book, Local Motors is given as an example. And their premise of smaller fabrication facilities, in my opinion, is spot on. Design globally and produce locally. Until recently, additive manufacturing has been still slower than many bulk processes such as casting, but the increasing speed, as well as the quality produced and the ability to custom design for 3D printing, changes the landscape. Not only can we now design parts that can be manufactured only by additive techniques, the first production-scale metal printing systems can also compete on cost. The result: increased strength, reduced weight, improvements in performance. In chapter 2, the authors provide some examples such as an aircraft bracket. Every day we are seeing new examples of this potential being unlocked, with benefits throughout the value chain.

Where do we go from here? In this book, the authors discuss the expanded innovation landscape and how it exhibits four different modes of innovation. Companies need to learn to navigate this new landscape and try new modes of innovation. Each mode requires its own managerial logic but also offers tremendous opportunity for firms, both large and small, new and established. Over the next 10 years, firms will embrace this notion of choosing to play in certain innovation modes, of moving between them over time or purposefully exploring multiple modes in parallel.

We live in a time of rapid change, creating challenges but also hope. The new technologies my firm and others are working on will make the world a better place, enabling solutions ranging from instantly produced, customized medical implants to safer airplanes. It will allow us to shift from centralized manufacturing in low-cost regions requiring carbon-emitting shipping over tens of thousands of miles toward more sustainable, local manufacturing and to shift from large payloads launched into orbit to on-demand fabrication of components in space. The future is coming – and fast. But innovators need to be prepared and embrace – to learn to navigate – this new landscape. Godspeed!

The
Innovation
Navigator

Introduction

Over 30 years ago, in 1986, Hirotaka Takeuchi and Ikujiro Nonaka, two Japanese management scholars, recommended that firms replace their old, sequential process with a new approach – rugby-style, passing the "ball" within the team down the field.[1] They called it the "new new product development game." It was a call to action for firms to reinvent their innovation process. Firms rightfully focused on cross-functional teams and Japanese-style management tools and techniques: a house of quality for everyone. This was followed by other approaches, such as quality management via Six Sigma and Black Belts, disruptive innovation, and more recently design thinking. Despite all of these important initiatives, tools, techniques, and consultants' advice, many firms still struggle with their innovation efforts. In fact, the failure rate of new products and services remains essentially unchanged – since 1968![2] Depending on the study, the failure rate for newly launched products and services hovers around 40 percent.[3] And even highly successful firms, like Ford and Apple, go through periods and cycles of reinvigorating their innovation process, then falling back with a return to bad habits. As we prepare for the third decade of the twenty-first century and what will certainly be a dynamic and challenging time for companies, we clearly need to look at the entirety of the innovation landscape and strategically think about our approach to innovation and how it can be improved – i.e., better innovations commercialized more quickly.

The challenges facing today's firms are unique. To use a fishing analogy, a successful commercial fishing boat can alter where and how it trolls for fish. Navigation paths, improved imaging technology, line sets, and duration can be modified to increase the catch. But environment and weather play a role in the boat's tactical approach, and like a storm tide formed by two meteorological forces (strong winds swirling toward the center of the storm, combined with low-pressure water currents), the way we approach the innovation game has been radically reshaped by two forces in recent years. They have created an expanded innovation landscape that has led to far-reaching changes in how companies can conceive, develop, and commercialize new products and services.

The emergence of digital design and a collaborative culture have fundamentally altered how firms, and people, approach the innovation process. In the pre–digital design era, most new product and service development was conducted by individuals and organizations holding the relevant expertise, and most collaboration either occurred inside of firms or was governed by market-based transactions between firms. Today, aided by digital design and fabrication tools on the one hand and social networking communities and collaboration/sharing tools on the other, the "innovation landscape" is marked by new forms of participation and ownership, with new participants entering new markets and new arrangements of collective innovation. The two major forces – digital design and a collaborative culture – form a "perfect storm" that substantially expands the innovation landscape, and in this new innovation landscape four distinct regions are emerging. Each of these regions calls for its own innovation management approach (i.e., its own innovation modus operandi). Each of these innovation modes comes with different but significant ramifications for users, consumers, communities, vendors, and firms themselves. The locus of expertise is shifting from the human expert to the tools, allowing the experts to push technology frontiers outward in the traditional regions of the new innovation landscape, while enabling non-experts to participate in some activities like never before, especially in the venture and community modes. At the same time, whereas economic transactions will remain the main form of exchange in the traditional regions, they are complemented by social exchanges in the other modes, especially the community mode, with significant challenges for designing incentives and ownership regimes.

The good news, of course, is that this creates an opportunity-rich environment for firms to innovate. The expanded landscape, and the new innovation modes that come with it, create an ecosystem where more ideas of higher quality can seed innovation funnels, where new engineering tools allow the vetting of more mature concepts earlier in the process, where new actors can help develop solutions, and where innovation networks can lower costs and barriers to entry. This means more ideas from more sources, the potential for better ideas, and ways to radically reduce the investment needed to bring them to market. The bad news is that this also creates some new demands and hurdles. Managers need frameworks for navigating and understanding how to harness the power of this new landscape. In this book we attempt to show that there are many opportunities to leverage this new landscape, but all four innovation modes exhibit their challenges. We encourage firms to explore these different modes but to do so with clear expectations and a firm grasp of the risk and reward potential.

But First, a Little Background

Both of us started out as mechanical engineers, and as such we were always interested in how things are designed and made. It is our view that how you approach the design of things, from the tools you use to the interactions of designers and engineers, is an all-important component to the ultimate success of any project – just as important as understanding the customer or spotting an untapped market. When we first met at a conference at MIT in 2005, we talked a lot about how computer-aided design (CAD) and other tools are really changing the way the engineers, the people down in the engineering bullpen, innovate. These new tools were changing long-established behaviors, and beyond noting that they could do really neat things and had the potential to transform the design process, we wondered what the true impact would be on innovation as a whole.

Up until that time, the design process of things had not been radically altered. Yes, CAD was used by most firms by the 1980s, but many of the ways teams proceeded through the steps of design and engineering were really no different than in the 1950s. And it worked well. The Boeing 747 went from idea to first flight in less than five years using slide rules and drafting boards. The 777, the first virtually designed plane for Boeing, was a highly successful project. The 787, on the other hand, was radically different in approach than its two older siblings, but also went radically over budget and schedule. The approach to the work changed, and we wanted to learn more, both about the upside and the possible downside.

So we set about over the next 10 years to understand changes to the innovation process, driven by tools and culture that in turn drove changes in the engineering and design organization. This book draws on a series of studies investigating how changes in design tool use and organizational structure affect innovation practices and performance. In this research, we investigated product development phenomena in small start-ups and large, established organizations, inside traditional organizational structures, as well as across recently emerging communities; and we explored the effects of modern design and communication tools across these settings. More specifically, we conducted detailed, longitudinal studies of how increased use of the CAD tools affects workload distribution across innovation phases and ultimately innovation performance. In concert with academic colleagues and an industry partner, we conducted two large empirical studies to investigate the use of design tools and the use of social media tools, both in established organizations. The first study included 122 firms; the second 198 firms. These studies focused on the use of digital design tools, team communication and collaboration, the use of social media, and the impact of outside contributors to the new product development (NPD) process. We also conducted in-depth interviews with founders and managers in start-ups and with C-level executives in large organizations. We talked to vendors, engineers, and academics.

As we developed our ideas, we presented and discussed our work for this book with colleagues at a number of academic conferences for several years. In addition, we developed an innovation simulation that further helped us sharpen our thinking about the question of how to navigate innovation. Finally, two combined academic and industry conferences specifically dedicated to product development collaboration and open innovation were developed and run at one of our home institutions. Multiple C-level executives and leading academics participated in presentations and discussion panels. Collectively, this research represents a comprehensive investigation into the changing landscape of innovation.

In the end, we developed our frameworks to help managers and executives take advantage of the tremendous opportunities that present themselves in each of the new modes of innovation. In the next chapter we discuss some history behind the development of the two forces which are expanding the innovation landscape. Then we dive into the innovation modes, with an eye toward giving practical advice on how to approach the unique benefits and challenges of each mode. Finally, we discuss how firms can use these modes together to great effect.

We hope this book helps readers navigate the storms that have arisen with these recent technological revolutions.

The Calm Waters of the Past: Managing Innovation in Organizations in the Twentieth Century

Firms today are overwhelmed with processes, gates, paperwork, and project leads, all designed to manage innovation: from Toyota's TPS (Toyota Production System) and Ford's GPDS (Global Product Development System) to Apple's DRI (Directly Responsible Individual). How did we get here? We need to provide a little historical context. If you look at the industrial giants of the twentieth century, many started out in the second half of the nineteenth century. In the United States, the time of rapid geographic and economic expansion after the Civil War was ripe with opportunity, and many individuals built technological solutions and founded companies that are well-known today: for example, General Electric (Thomas Edison), Ford Motor Company (Henry Ford), and Standard Oil (John D. Rockefeller). In the twentieth century all these companies expanded both geographically and into new product markets. As a result, most of these organizations developed organizational structures and management processes, and many grew into a multidivisional structure to reduce the decision-making load at the top management level and to shift decisions into the divisions that were closer to the market.[1]

In this larger organizational context, innovation became a function within most organizations, just as manufacturing, purchasing, or human resources are. Many companies created units whose role it was to research new technologies and develop next-generation products and sometimes services. Edison's Menlo Park industrial research laboratory in New Jersey became one of the most famous of these research and development (R&D) units. While technologies and the innovations themselves progressed at an amazing pace throughout the last century, innovation as an activity remained for the most part the responsibility of dedicated R&D units for most of the twentieth century. The management of these units was embedded in the larger hierarchical decision-making process. In other words, strategic decisions from top management led to the identification of promising technical areas. Once identified, these problems (or opportunities) became the focus of the R&D departments, and they began to develop solutions for these problems. The top-level management decisions cascaded down the organization, indicating which projects would receive resources and which engineer was assigned to which project. In other words, the task allocation and resource control followed the corporate hierarchical structure. Minor changes to the process notwithstanding, innovation management in most large firms still functions today using this model. This is even true for most of the latest generation of corporate giants, such as Apple, Microsoft, and even Facebook.

Consider a generic innovation process model as shown in Figure 1.1. It consists of two sets of diverging and converging processes (that's why it is often called the "double-diamond"). The first diamond represents a search for problems or opportunities. This search might be pursued consciously or it might be considered outside of one's control, the problem being handed down from management or forced upon a team by a market competitor. In the

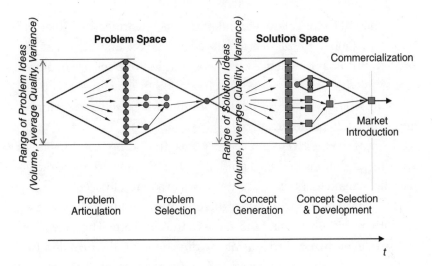

Figure 1.1: Innovation process model.
© 2018 Tucker J. Marion, Sebastian K. Fixson

broadest terms, the problem search includes a divergent phase in which possible problems and opportunities are considered to be worthwhile and deserving attention and resources, followed by some form of selection decision, as no organization has sufficient resources to work on all problems or opportunities it theoretically could work on. Because these selection decisions have resource allocation consequences, they are often made at higher levels in the organization. In most large organizations today, upper management or some form of steering committee decides which technologies to focus on and where to spend research dollars to develop new solutions. For example, in a large car manufacturer with multiple brands and models, a steering committee with representatives from all brands meets at regular intervals to review the technologies in the R&D pipeline, to evaluate the projects' progress, and to allocate resources for the next period.

The actual technical development then is illustrated in the second diamond. Once a problem is identified as a target, another divergent process unfolds in which a variety of solution options are explored (some of which are developed) before another convergent step follows, in which a small number of solutions is selected, developed, and ultimately commercialized.

For most of the twentieth century this process occurred inside of large organizations and was guided by the hierarchy that characterizes the management of most enterprises in a market-based economy. The owner of a company, either directly or via holding shares, tasks executives with increasing the value of the company. The executives in turn develop and devise strategic directions for the firm and cascade these down subsequent layers of management. The internal R&D policy in most large organizations has followed this pattern: strategic direction is provided by senior leadership, and managers design and execute projects to further the goals of this strategy.

The management of these processes followed the logic developed during the first industrial revolution. Just as the father of industrial engineering, Frederick Taylor, and his contemporaries began to measure factory work and designed it to be executed in an optimized way according to the principles of scientific management,[2] R&D was organized in separate units inside of large organizations. And while the pendulum between central R&D units and R&D inside divisional structures swung to the latter with the appearance of very large organizations by the mid-twentieth century,[3] the internal logic of how R&D units are run remained unchanged.

Looking at the features of innovation management in the organizations that the Industrial Revolution spawned 150 years ago, and which we can see still today at the beginning of the twenty-first century, three sets of key parameters can be identified. The firms that manage these parameters more effectively and efficiently have tended to identify and select better problems to work on and solve them in a fashion that leads to higher financial rewards. One set of critical parameters considers task allocation – in other words, who does what. Whereas before the Industrial Revolution the roles of designer, maker, and user were often occupied by a single individual, industrialization triggered rapid specializations of tasks, which led to the separation of the roles of the designer and manufacturer of a product from the role of the end user. This role split not only is prevalent in industry today but can also be found in most product development process models.[4] With the product development expertise now residing inside of manufacturing companies, new communication channels such as marketing had to be established to learn about the needs of the user population. In turn, the users – many of whom have benefited from the productivity improvement through higher wages, which collectively allowed the formation of a consuming middle class – became disengaged from the design and manufacturing of the goods that they acquired and consumed. The acceleration of knowledge development, the investment in time and money to acquire specific knowledge (school, apprenticeship), and the concentration of ownership of production equipment has further increased this role separation over time. In sum, the task allocation in most modern innovation processes can be described as an organizational design that has internal specialists engaging in designing and making products and external consumers using and consuming them.

Another set of critical parameters is concerned with ownership or access control. This second set of parameters is related but not identical to the first. Instead of describing who does the work, it specifies who owns what, or more specifically, who controls access to the relevant resources and expertise. Inside most market-based firms and organizations, firm ownership confers decision rights, and these are used to direct work. In this sense, in most traditional firms, the ownership or access control is the force that enables task allocations within and between enterprises. Intellectual property in the form of patents, copyrights, or trademarks is another form of ownership or access control, here extended to intangible items.

Finally, whereas organizational design and resource control tend to be longer-term decisions, the third set of critical parameter focuses on tactical and operational aspects: the key performance indicators (KPIs) and consequently incentives for the stakeholders involved. In most commercial organizations, innovation activities are ultimately measured by their contribution to the business, often assessed as sales performance. On the project level, this overarching goal is often subdivided into sub-goals as time-to-market, cost-to-market, product quality, and unit cost. In recent years, customization has become another factor.

These three sets of parameters allow us to understand how innovation work has been organized. The traditional form of innovation management is not going to go away, but major changes in technology and society are expanding the innovation management landscape and thus making new modes of managing innovation possible, and in some circumstances even preferable. These new modes can act as different levers in the innovation process (Figure 1.1) and can affect not only the quality and quantity of problems and solutions but also traditional project KPIs. The parameters introduced in this chapter will allow us to show how innovation management can be organized differently. But first, let's look at the forces that create the storm.

Technological and Social Change Create the "Perfect Storm" for Innovation

We are in the midst of a second industrial revolution. And just as the first industrial revolution 200 years ago brought dramatic changes in both technical and social dimensions, this second industrial revolution is also changing the way we design, make, and use products and services. In other words, the landscape that characterizes innovation management processes is significantly expanding. Two major forces – one technical and one social – are driving this change: digital design and a collaborative culture. Not only is each force powerful in its own right, but they also reinforce each other to create a perfect storm. Let's look at them and their interaction in detail.

Force 1: Digital Design

The technical force that contributes to the emerging innovation landscape, digital design,[1] is itself a combination of two factors: the rapid performance improvements of computers over the past 60 years and the increasing sophistication of digital design and manufacturing tools over the past 30 years (we deliberately include both the design and the manufacturing part).

The performance improvements of computers over the past six decades resulting from technical developments are absolutely remarkable. For example, when compared with human computing 150 years ago, computer performance has increased by a factor somewhere between 1.7 trillion and 76 trillion, depending on the measurement standard. Most of this astonishing progress occurred between World War II and today, resulting in an average rate of improvement of 45 percent per year (!) and an associated reduction in cost per calculation.[2] This phenomenal increase in computing power has led to the use of computers in many applications, ranging from airplanes, cars, and machines to phones, appliances, watches, and many more.

Similarly, software programs supporting design and manufacturing activities have made dramatic progress over the past 30 years. For example, while the origins of computer-aided design tools go back to the 1950s, it took 20 more years for commercially packaged CAD software to appear on the market (until then most CAD system development work was conducted inside large automotive and aerospace companies). During the 1980s parametric modeling tools and 3D modeling were introduced, and in the 1990s CAD systems became available that could run on a personal computer, no longer requiring expensive workstations. At the same time, the cost of CAD systems continually fell over the past 30 years (to the point that in 2018 some versions are free), and their performance and user-friendliness have drastically increased.[3] Today, many CAD programs provide substantial tutorials that allow fast learning curves, even for novices and children. In other words, the locus of expertise has moved, to a large degree, to the tool itself. As a result, the barrier for almost anyone to design products has become remarkably low. Similar developments are evident for other computer-aided engineering analysis tools used for tasks such as FEA (finite element analysis).

As with the design tools, computer-aided and computer-controlled manufacturing tools have developed dramatically over the past 30 years. Initially, digitization led to numerically controlled (NC) versions of existing machine tools, such as lathes, saws, and mills; later these became computer numerically controlled (CNC). But the ability to digitally control various manufacturing processes also led to the development of entirely new processes. For example, during this same period, various rapid prototyping technologies have progressed to a point that today they offer in the form of additive manufacturing technologies, also often labeled as 3D-printing, a mechanism that allows the fabrication of parts in almost any geometry in a batch size of one.[4] Similar to CAD, the capabilities of these technologies have substantially increased and their costs have dramatically declined. While currently still more expensive on a unit-cost basis than mass production technologies for large production volumes, these new digital manufacturing processes open up small-batch production that was hitherto economically impossible and often technologically infeasible. This, in turn, has two consequences: first, it makes it possible for almost anyone to manufacture a product, or to have it manufactured, through low-cost internet-based 3D printing and rapid prototyping services, so-called service bureaus; and second, it enables the design and fabrication of far superior solutions. The independence from fixed tooling also means that much of the expertise for making parts and systems has moved to the tool itself. These trends continue to accelerate, with new firms like Formlabs (www.formlabs.com) commercializing increasingly capable and low-cost 3D-printing solutions.

More generally speaking, digitization is dramatically accelerating a trend from moving the locus of expertise from humans to tools. Historically, the expertise resided with specific individuals. Over time, expertise became codified and more widely distributed (think books and manuals), enabling novices to engage in more sophisticated tasks. Digitization is accelerating this diffusion of expertise from humans to tools such that many tools and even products now have the expertise built-in (think computers, many software-based analysis tools, or automobiles).

Force 2: Collaborative Culture

The other force contributing to the major change of the innovation landscape is a social phenomenon. Children born in the 1980s and 1990s, sometimes called Generation Y or millennials, grew up as "digital natives": not only were they raised with the internet and a vast array of digital tools, but they are also accustomed to a culture of collaboration and sharing that differs from that of previous generations.[5] True, another technical innovation, the internet, has fueled this development. In the United States, the portion of adults who use the internet jumped from about 52 percent in 2000 to 88 percent in 2016.[6] But it is not just the increased use of technical tools that distinguishes this generation from previous ones; their behavior also differs. Millennials are more likely to collaborate across time zones and geographic distances, and as consumers they are more interested in services and experiences than ownership.[7]

This culture is visible in communication behavior, in the way and the degree to which communities (both face-to-face and online) are formed, and in the formation of new types of business that combine hierarchical and community aspects. Consider companies such as Airbnb or Uber, the poster children of the so-called sharing economy.

In professional arenas, large communities have emerged, frequently online, in which people collaborate, often with minimal or sometimes even without exchange of direct economic value (i.e., money) and without traditional hierarchical controls (e.g., the open-source software community).

Two Forces Combining for the Perfect Storm

The two forces of digital design and collaborative culture are very powerful each in their own right, but their joint occurrence generates a "perfect storm"; that is, the individual forces combine and reinforce each other such that the whole is more than the sum of its parts (Figure 2.1). Digital design tools such as CAD make the use of rapid prototyping easier. Modern CAD programs not only create digital files describing the geometry of a component, their original purpose, but also allow easy conversion into file formats (e.g., STL) that rapid prototyping machines can read. For example, the latest SolidWorks CAD software has a function that reads simply "3D print," just as word processing programs have a function called "print." Likewise, the fact that 3D-printing processes do not create the same manufacturing-process-induced limitations that many traditional fabrication processes do, allows the generation of entirely new geometries in the CAD programs. Because CAD models are simply digital files, they can be easily transmitted and shared in digital repositories (e.g., GrabCAD, Dropbox). In turn, the sharing culture motivates users to collaborate on design projects, perhaps by modifying, mashing, or hacking the same CAD model stored remotely in file-sharing services, wikis, or communication platforms in the cloud (e.g., Dropbox, Basecamp, Slack). Finally, the independence of rapid prototyping technologies from its application area promotes its use in service form (software as a service, or SAAS) such that a user can not only hire prototyping capacity on demand (e.g., with a service provider such as Stratasys Direct Manufacturing),

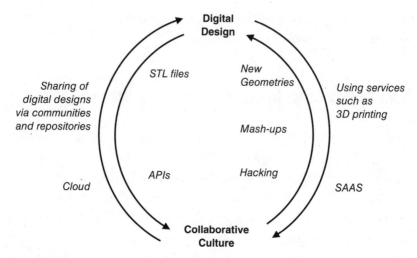

Figure 2.1: Perfect storm of digital and collaborative forces.
© 2018 Tucker J. Marion, Sebastian K. Fixson

but also plug in other applications via APIs (application programming interfaces). On the low end, communities build their own 3D printers by hacking (improving the printers of others).

Effects on the Innovation Landscape

As mentioned earlier, in the pre–digital design era, the innovation landscape exhibited a clearly identifiable mode in which traditional, market-facing organizations internally developed new products and services. What the combination of digital design and fabrication tools on one hand and social networking and new forms of collaboration and sharing on the other have done to this traditional mode of innovation is caused a substantial expansion of the innovation landscape, which is now significantly larger and more diverse (Figure 2.2).

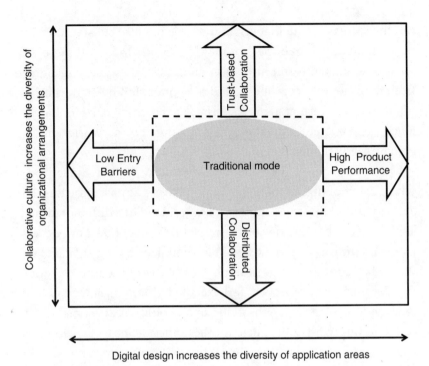

Figure 2.2: Innovation landscape expansion.
© 2016 Tucker J. Marion, Sebastian K. Fixson

The performance improvement of digital design tools has expanded the innovation landscape in two separate directions. On the high-performance end, the new tools enable the development of technical solutions that have previously been impossible. Consider, for example, the ability of modern CAD tools to assess the product's later performance in use through built-in tools such as finite element analysis (FEA), or to assess its manufacturability through mold-flow analysis in the case of injection-molded components. Industrial versions of 3D printing allow creation of new geometries that are substantially lighter than parts produced with standard manufacturing processes, an invaluable advantage in the aerospace industry.

But the increasing intelligence of the tools has also substantially improved the user-friendliness of the CAD tools. Today, all these systems operate with graphical user interfaces that users recognize from their own PCs or tablets, and they offer step-by-step tutorials, often in video format. This lowering of the entry barriers has enabled people to enter the design and manufacturing world without being experts themselves.

The second force, the collaborative culture, in part fueled by a whole array of digital tools that make sharing almost effortless, has also expanded the innovation landscape, albeit in a different dimension. It has reshaped how and why people collaborate. For one, distributed innovation needs to leverage digital technology to its fullest, which has contributed to how physically distributed new product development is approached and executed.[8] Many firms today have work processes that span the globe, and people have become used to collaborating with colleagues in other offices, cities, or even countries. In addition to spanning multiple units within a company or a supply chain, work also increasingly occurs in decentralized organizational structures, often called communities. Participants in these communities are driven by a mix of intrinsic and extrinsic motivations, and the collaboration is often guided through trust and norm-based interactions rather than the command-and-control actions that are typical within hierarchical organizations.

This expanded innovation management landscape can be characterized by four different innovation modes. In the following chapters, we introduce our framework to map out the expanded innovation landscape and discuss these modes in detail. We explain how companies operate in them, as well as the challenges and opportunities they provide to those companies active in these modes. In later chapters we also explore the questions of dynamic moves between innovation modes and multimode strategies.

The Four Modes of Innovation
in the Digital Era

In the last chapter, we explored the "perfect storm" of two forces that have forever changed the landscape of how we innovate. In looking at the last 20 years, it is clear that new forms of sharing and collaboration combined with ever more capable and accessible digital design tools allow more people to be involved in the innovation process at different times. The combination of changes in tools and culture allows companies to explore different forms of organizational structure and, hence, tap into different sources of innovation. This in turn impacts who does what, how they are compensated, and who owns the intellectual property. For firms, this goes to the heart of how new products and services are developed and commercialized.

With the technical force enabling significant performance improvements for some and lowering the barriers to entry for others, and the social force extending the sets of possible organizational forms by including collaborative and virtual arrangements, the innovation landscape is now much larger and more diverse than ever before. The "perfect storm" occurring at the beginning of the twenty-first century has resulted in the emergence of four unique modes of innovation, which we label *specialist*, *venture*, *community*, and

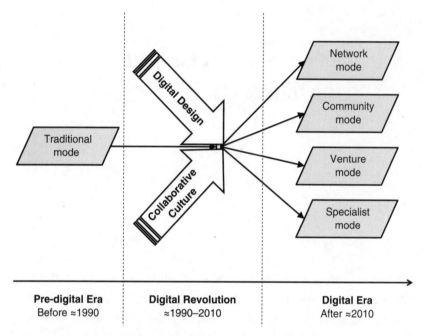

Figure 3.1: Two forces create four new innovation modes.
© 2016 Tucker J. Marion, Sebastian K. Fixson

network (see Figure 3.1). Each innovation mode is characterized by its own set of stakeholders and interaction dynamics. These different modes have developed and matured since the "perfect storm," and firms need to understand the DNA – the internal makeup – of each mode and where and when they can be used most effectively.

To lay out and better describe the expanded innovation landscape, we developed the framework shown in Figure 3.2. We will use this framework as a basis for discussing each mode and the strategies required for exploring and navigating to new modes.

Along the horizontal axis we define the organizational scope of the framework. On the left side of the axis are those projects that

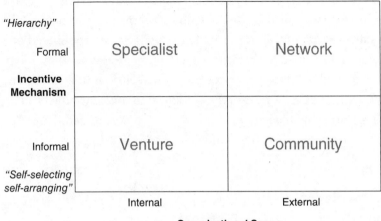

Figure 3.2: The innovation mode framework.
© 2018 Tucker J. Marion, Sebastian K. Fixson.

predominantly rely on internal resources. These projects are typically performed by internal R&D teams, both large and small. On the right side are those projects that involve external resources, from individuals to established vendors. These projects typically cross traditional firm boundaries.

The vertical axis of the framework represents a range of incentive mechanisms, separated by the degree of formality. For the specialist and network modes, the incentives to organize and produce are well defined and quantified, and they are directed to specific employees and partners. Think of a strategic business unit's operating plan for growth and profitability or the contract agreement with a supplier. At the bottom of the vertical axis, the method of incentive is less formal and includes intrinsic motivation rather than a straightforward incentive structure (monetary or otherwise). These incentives are often set to trigger a self-selection mechanism, in contrast to the more formal way of directing specific work to specific people. An internal venture may start out with an engaged and motivated employee who, during a portion of their work time that they themselves control, creates a new solution to a self-identified problem. This idea underlies, for example, Google's "20 percent time" rule.

Let's now look at each of the innovation modes in detail and discuss the opportunities and challenges presented by each.

The Specialist Mode

The performance improvements enabled through digital design are primarily responsible for the specialist mode of the expanded innovation landscape. It is the closest descendant of established new product development from the pre-digital era. In this mode, we often see complex projects that are primarily driven by for-profit organizations, with specialized expertise in their given industries. These often high-risk, high-reward projects are typically developed and commercialized by formal organizations, using either hierarchy (in-house) or markets (outsourced) as organizing mechanisms. Companies such as Volkswagen and Samsung Electronics are firms active in this mode. Here's an example of how the specialist mode operates. Consider an aerospace firm that uses advanced digital design and rapid prototyping fabrication technology to push the performance frontier for its products to new levels. Figure 3.3 shows a redesigned structural component that provides similar strength at a significantly lower part weight. The true innovation lies in the fact that the new component could not have been produced with traditional part fabrication technologies but was 3D-printed instead. Specialists adopt these new technologies to improve their

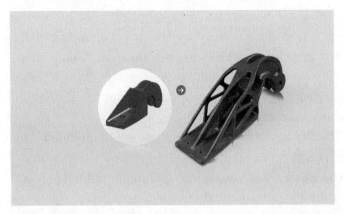

Figure 3.3: Example for weight reduction of high-performance components. Source: EADS.

designs and resulting competitive advantage. The example shown in Figure 3.3 is an airplane component from Airbus/EADS. The titanium bracket on the right side of Figure 3.3 has been optimized for a 3D-printed manufacturing process (laser sintering).

Specialists do not have to be long-established companies. Startups that focus on employing advanced digital design tools to shift performance frontiers can also operate in this mode. An example is the aerospace venture SpaceX, which is experimenting with new ways to interact with and manipulate the digital models of its rocket and spacecraft designs.

Opportunities and Challenges

The opportunities for firms operating in the specialist mode present themselves in creating new products and services by pushing the envelope of product performance. Technical possibilities also open up entirely new application areas, such as the use of 3D scanning and printing of human body parts for surgery preparation and training. The combination of tools and collaborative sharing can also lead to enhancement in the process itself. Some firms are increasingly experimenting with "always on" or live large video portals, allowing more natural and relaxed insight and communication with distributed offices.

The challenges in the specialist mode are to build these technical capabilities in-house so that they are harder for competitors to imitate. The market is already placing a premium on this aspect. One recent example is the increasing financial incentives Apple and Tesla are each offering for employees of the other firm to join theirs instead. Attracting, developing, and retaining highly skilled technical personnel are key elements to the long-term success of a specialist.

In various industries, firms are taking steps to insource design and manufacturing to further strengthen core competencies and competitive advantage. Examples range from computer manufacturers such as Apple who develop their own central processing unit (CPU) microprocessors to automotive firms such as Tesla designing and assembling their own battery packs and motors for electric vehicles. In case the capabilities have to be sought outside the company, one of the key challenges is to create the appropriate incentives and contracts for inter-company innovation.

Another challenge in the specialist mode is the need for judicious process management of tool use itself. While the digital design and fabrication tools can indeed improve the productivity of many activities – for example, testing and iteration – they tend not to do that automatically but rather benefit from appropriate process management.[1] Near photo-realistic early digital designs may offer a false sense of project completeness while the ease of iteration can lead to unnecessary design churn. Executives need to encourage and empower adoption of these tools while making sure their R&D

managers maintain process discipline. In terms of communication and collaboration technologies, the benefits are clear. Recent research has shown that companies that use social-media-centric collaboration technologies (e.g., project wikis) outperform those that do not.[2] For distributed R&D teams, increased connection and communication are essential.

The Venture Mode

The venture mode of the expanded innovation landscape broadens the class of participants to include even more actors, many of whom could not have entered the marketplace or considered being a part of the innovation process even 10 years ago. This mode has been made possible by modern digital design tools lowering the entry barriers. Actors in this mode tend to assemble the necessary resources by using intermediate services that provide access to specialized tools and skills. As an example of a firm operating in the venture mode, consider the start-up company U-Turn Audio (uturnaudio.com). Three students in Boston founded this new venture in 2012. They were able to leverage digital design tools and access low-cost rapid prototyping and suppliers of low-volume, low-cost manufacturing (e.g., 100kgarages.com) to develop a high-quality, reasonably priced vinyl long-play (LP) turntable for a growing audiophile niche market (Figure 3.4). To fund their effort, they turned to the online crowdfunding site Kickstarter to raise over $200,000. They used these funds and local low-volume manufacturers to resolve design issues and purchase trial production parts. The combination of rapid prototypes, quick-turn preproduction parts, and off-the-shelf components was assembled by the founding team in Boston. This allowed the team to gain valuable

Figure 3.4: New venture U-Turn Audio's product, the Orbit.
Source: U-Turn Audio.

insights from lead customers and refine the design in near real time. As they transitioned to fulfilling customer orders, the team moved to a small manufacturing facility and is currently producing units for a growing customer base.

Because new and nimble entrants like U-Turn mostly do not own the equipment or the assets they need to get off the ground, an entire ecosystem of various economic actors has emerged to support these new participants. Some provide design tools (e.g., Google Sketch-Up or Onshape) or design libraries (e.g., Thingiverse.com), others offer 3D-printing services for various materials (e.g., Shapeways, 3D Systems) or access to fabrication options (e.g., Makersrow.com, 100kgarages.com), others offer help in finding and selecting suppliers (e.g., MFG.com, Alibaba.com), and yet others aid in demonstrating market viability and fundraising (e.g., Kickstarter, Indiegogo).

As an example for these new service companies, consider Makerspace (makerspace.com). Makerspaces bring people and tools together to develop projects or prototypes. These spaces connect inventors, entrepreneurs, craftsmen, and students to coalesce around specialized interests with the goal of making an object or prototype and often to start new businesses.

Opportunities and Challenges

The venture mode clearly offers opportunities for both small start-ups and large corporations seeking to become more entrepreneurial. For innovation managers of more established firms, this mode can allow small entrepreneurial teams to develop new product ideas and test them at low cost. These internal "start-up" teams can help seed traditional concept funnels with ideas that are more advanced in terms of design and concept testing than traditional methods. Existing innovation teams can also become more "lean" by using the techniques of resource-constrained new ventures.[3]

One challenge for firms active in the venture mode is that the ability to quickly identify, select, and assemble necessary resources in itself is a required skill.[4] These markets are often moving fast, and the ability to protect the business through intellectual property is often limited, so the most powerful competitive advantage is high velocity. In other words, those who can assemble resources fastest without actually owning them win. Another challenge is the ability to build scale into the design itself. Working prototypes or extremely low-volume crafted products are not necessarily designed for mass production and mass profits. If business model scalability is ultimately important to the individual or firm, design and manufacturing scalability needs to be considered as well. For service providers active in this innovation mode, one challenge is the question of how to find scalable, non-niche markets. Many of the service providers benefit from network effects, so in some sub-areas of this region there might not be space for many rivals.

The Community Mode

The third mode of the new innovation landscape attracts large numbers of new entrants due to the low barriers of entry and includes – at least in part – a trust-based form of organizing. For this reason, we label this mode "community." In this mode, the setting of organizational and decision-making boundaries becomes substantially more "fuzzy," as collaborating with like-minded strangers becomes an integral part for some business models. In other words, some transactions in this region are not guided primarily by either markets or hierarchies. Instead, sharing exchanges and voluntary contributions become part of the repertoire. Relatively low-complexity products, collaboratively designed by communities of hobbyists or individuals with a keen motivation and interest in the intellectual and emotional (and sometimes monetary) pursuits of miscellaneous projects, exemplify this innovation mode. An example of a for-profit company in this region is Quirky (quirky.com). Quirky established a community of over one million participants who aid in the suggesting, selecting, and designing of new products. The community included a large variety of expertise and interest levels, although the community was not a professional network per se. The economic model was a variation of licensing, in which the community selects and designs the inventor's product, and contributing members in return earn small monetary rewards if the product is commercialized. The products were primarily low-complexity consumer products, sold online or through large retailers.

For example, on November 7, 2010, an individual inventor submitted the idea of an improved ice scraper for car windows to Quirky's website. After a week of commenting and voting by the community, the idea entered the on-site (but live-streamed on the web) product evaluation and was selected for further development. The community continued to be involved through multiple sub-projects around product function, industrial design, naming and tag-lining, and pricing – all web-based – in which participants earned influence points for their participation. Getting the design production-ready and onto retailers' shelves was accomplished by Quirky staff. The product, the ice scraper Thor, went on sale on November 23, 2011. The company maintained, monitored, and curated the various forums in which the community discussed product ideas as well as various process dimensions such as evaluation criteria and the influence-point allocation formula. The lively discussion around the products suggested a strong emotional connection between many community members and Quirky.[5]

This form of distributed collaboration for new product development is a relatively new space, and it attracted a great deal of attention and financial capital. Quirky received over $150 million in venture capital investment over the life of the first iteration of the company. A schematic of their innovation process is shown in Figure 3.5.

Opportunities and Challenges

The opportunities for firms operating in this mode are potentially new forms of market development and user engagement. The idea of open innovation clearly resonates in both academic and business circles, as many firms have experimented or are planning to experiment with open innovation initiatives. Both new ideas from and

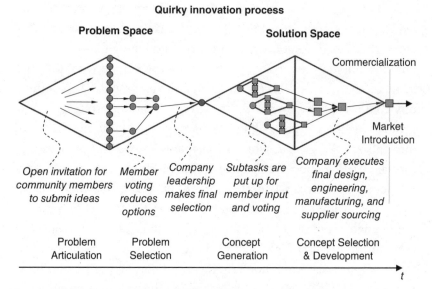

Figure 3.5: Example of a social product development process.
© 2018 Tucker J. Marion, Sebastian K. Fixson

closer ties with consumers can be the result. For this very reason, General Electric (GE) invested $30 million in Quirky and opened up a portion of its patent portfolio to their user community in 2013.[6]

At the same time, several challenges are also present in this mode. For example, the decision-making authority of the owners of a firm might be more constrained if the opinions of one million community members have to be considered. This can be especially challenging when the community's needs have to be balanced with other business considerations. For example, Quirky's development of an app-enabled air-conditioning window unit in collaboration with GE Appliances led to an accelerated development schedule. The consequence: some decisions were made without involving the community, leading to considerable discontent among many community members. In addition, maintaining a viable and contributing community over time is no simple feat and may require substantial resources to manage, with careful considerations of the type and scope of incentives. Finally, viable business models in which people pay for small volume production – i.e., the opposite of scale – may be difficult to find. In fact, in February 2015, Quirky announced a reduction of categories it pursued under its own name while increasing the number of collaborations with existing brands for other categories, such as Harman (audio) and Mattel (toys). In September 2015, Quirky declared bankruptcy but has emerged since as Quirky 2.0. Clearly, the open innovation community established by Quirky was a powerful concept to both participants and financiers, even if the first version of its business model turned out to be flawed. This mode is still in its infancy, and firms need to be conscious of how implement a business model that is both sound and financially scalable.[7]

The Network Mode

The network mode crosses firm boundaries with directed innovation work relationships. This region combines a general requirement for substantial product design expertise with relationships typical in networks. These networks can include key technology suppliers, universities, and startups. Requirements for performance are high, and the integration of a distributed network of partners that are tasked with significant contributions to the overall innovation effort can be challenging. Perhaps because of the nature of this combination, until recently this has been the most uncharted of the modes. The Boeing 787 was an experiment in the network mode, with Boeing giving high levels of design authority over to major component and systems suppliers, allowing the aircraft's final assembly to occur in a manner similar to automobiles. A leader in this mode is Apple. Beginning with their alliance with Foxconn and close relationships with suppliers such as Hitachi and Corning, and extending to their developer network for apps, Apple is an example of a firm that has developed a tightly knit innovation ecosystem that relies heavily on innovation outside the walls of their offices in Cupertino.

Opportunities and Challenges

The opportunity in the network mode obviously lies in the chance to build an innovation system where the whole is more than the sum of its parts. Bringing together the expertise from a wide range of disciplines and geographies, supported and enabled by advanced digital tools, allows the emergence of entirely new solutions, potentially one which would never emerge in traditional organizational setups. If successfully managed, new product development in this mode can enable the creation of better product solutions and potential for improved processes. Rearranging organizational boundaries and new incentive structures are part of this opportunity.

The challenges lie in how to successfully develop and manage the processes, which require more coordination because of the greater levels of complexity. Building relationships and norms, ensuring sufficient overlap of (or at least information flow between) designer and partner organizations, and orchestrating the actual work are no easy tasks. We have seen the challenges firms have had with controlled, distributed development among suppliers (e.g., the Boeing 787), let alone thousands of individual contributors. Another important challenge in this mode – as well as in the community mode – is how to handle intellectual property questions while simultaneously maintaining the appropriate incentives for the participants. For example, an open-source vehicle that allows user variation may not have the same standardized quality control and safety that a manufacturer who has all or most processes in-house desires. This may in turn affect government regulations, warranty transferability, and product life cycles.

For innovation executives, the network mode – like the community mode – is an attractive area to investigate. One critical issue is the appropriate parsing of components and subsystems.[8] While it is straightforward to have a community give input on a mechanical bracket, it is another for these contributors to have visibility over an entire subsystem or total system. By eschewing strict control over suppliers on-site, Boeing experienced serious challenges in integrating critical subsystems of the 787. This contributed to the budget and schedule difficulties seen over the life of the project. Innovation managers, in considering this mode, need to be conscious of the critical issue of design and systems integration. Lastly, this mode, like the community mode, is dynamic, with many within the respective spaces changing business models and trying new approaches. Firms looking to explore this mode need to understand that paradigms of process and of interaction are still in their infancy and may change dramatically as these modes mature. For the opportunities and challenges of each innovation mode, a summary is shown in Table 3.1.

The Six Factors

As firms navigate to different modes, test new modes, or invest the time to operate in multiple modes, there are important factors

Table 3.1 Innovation Mode Opportunities and Challenges

Innovation Mode	Opportunities	Challenges
Specialist	New design tools allow advancing technology	Building capability internally
	New collaborative tools can spur process advances	Keeping superior personnel
Venture	Novices and resource-constrained projects can enter	Finding scalable projects and markets
	With new entrants, the markets for new services will grow	Design and manufacturing scalability
Community	Prospective customer involvement	Establishing sustainable and scalable business models
	Traditional open innovation benefits	Maintaining inflow of new participants
Network	Bundling expertise from different fields	Balancing external and intrinsic motivation
	Improved product solutions and process efficiencies	Increasing systems-level integration

to consider. As we looked at each mode and its inherent qualities and challenges, we returned to the three sets of critical parameters that we had identified in our analysis of current innovation management in chapter 1. Here we describe two factors for each of the sets that we consider critical. At the foundational level, thinking about the innovation process brings up important questions about resource ownership and control. Who is going to control the resources, from both a human and financial capital standpoint? That is, who is going to own the rights to the work? These questions must consider ownership rights to intangible assets such as patents and copyrights. These factors are represented as Level 1 in the Six Factors framework (see Figure 3.6). The next consideration

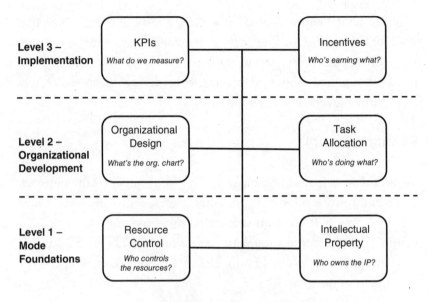

Roadmap for Mode Development

Figure 3.6: The Six Factors. © 2018 Tucker J. Marion, Sebastian K. Fixson

in mode development and management is how it affects the orga-nization. At the heart of this issue is the task allocation: Who does which part of the innovation work? Are they experts or lay-people? Do they work for your organization or another one? Or for none at all? How much do these choices impact the personnel and how they interact and are managed? Is the traditional organization chart radically altered?

Last, in thinking about implementation – where the rubber meets the road – how do you measure success? Are there new ways, be-yond traditional key performance metrics, that should be consid-ered? Whether you will be relying on suppliers, a community of engaged enthusiasts, or an internal corporate entrepreneur, how should they be compensated? Are there alternative incentives that are more impactful for these different actors? In each mode chapter, we will discuss these important considerations in detail. As you think about exploring new modes, considering these six factors across three levels will be essential.

Resource Control

Given the anticipated organizational scope changes of the network and community modes, how does this affect resource ownership and control? This will have an impact on agreements with suppliers, contracts, and relationships with community members. In addition, firms may release control of once closely held core competencies for the benefit of the network.

Intellectual Property (IP)

As firms' cross boundaries with individuals and the network, what role will intellectual property play? When digital designs can be shared and manipulated freely, by many, will traditional views of ownership and defense of IP rights change? Or will the focus on defending core technology become increasingly important? The sharing of Tesla's IP portfolio is an indication of one viewpoint; the battle between Samsung and Apple illustrates another.

Task Allocation

New forms of design and communication have changed the traditional role of who does what. Should we rely only on specialized individuals within the company as the generators of new ideas and entrepreneurial businesses, or should we consider everyone? Do we source critical systems and tasks to outside partners? Can we rely on outside communities to help internal engineering teams solve design challenges?

Organizational Design

In firms looking to adopt different modes of innovation, how will those decisions impact the organizational design of departments and business units? Will teams of the network mode co-locate? Will individual ventures be able to operate outside of normal processes, to be true corporate entrepreneurs?

Key Performance Indicators

Once tasks are reallocated and new organizational processes are created, as firms explore news modes, new key performance indicators for each will need to be developed. If the community can support millions of contributions, will the number of ideas become less important than the quality of those ideas? Will firms with defined venture modes need to adopt more entrepreneurial KPIs such as a focus on cash burn rates, time to break even, and venture-capital-like 7–10x returns?

Incentives

Beyond salary and other forms of compensation for actors involved in the innovation process, what is the true motivation for the firm and contributors? Each mode requires a different approach to incentives and a different definition of what these mean for employees, managers, and other collaborators. Is a Facebook community with volunteers enough to gain input for new product features? Or do you need a compensated, open innovation system where contributors are paid for contributing new ideas or evaluating new concepts?

Navigating the Expanded Landscape

For innovative firms, the new landscape is not static but rather a dynamic space in which to move or transition to. Firms are shifting modes and exploring new modes, often concurrently. Let's look at the case of Apple (Figure 3.7).

In 1976, Apple began as a new venture, gaining traction with their Apple II in the late 1970s, attracting venture capital investment, and ultimately transitioning to a specialist mode. With successive iterations of the Apple II and new product introductions such as the Macintosh in 1984, they became a Fortune 100 specialist. However, since then Apple has transitioned from being a specialist to being firmly rooted in the network mode. They rely heavily on their manufacturing partner Foxconn, they are at the center of a component ecosystem that drives supplier relationships, and they actively promote their developer network for iPhone, Watch, and Apple TV applications. Boeing also experimented with the network mode with the 787, moving from the specialist mode to apply network mode characteristics.

An important aspect to consider is the dynamism of the modes themselves. The new innovation modes are generally populated with firms and services that are new or relatively new start-ups. From GrabCAD to Makerbot, these firms and services can be ephemeral, as evidenced by the implosion of Quirky. For firms looking to explore these new modes, we suggest they develop an understanding of the risks involved by experimenting on a limited basis first. The initiatives need to have clear, succinct goals and

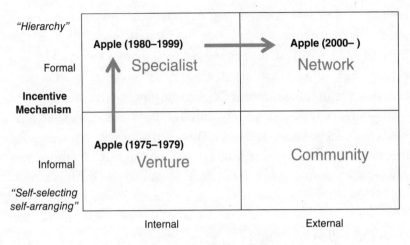

Figure 3.7: Mode dynamics. © 2018 Tucker J. Marion, Sebastian K. Fixson.

outcomes. Less successful are those that are too grand and have too little direction. Establishing a partnership with the local maker space and hoping for innovation may not be enough. However, identifying a specific market opportunity, engaging a community of enthusiasts, and giving employees the tools needed to quickly develop and vet concepts can be a powerful combination. Once the test is completed, the organization can seek to implement best practices in other business units.

Exploring New Modes

As firms investigate new modes, managers need to consider the important ramifications as they contemplate navigating the new landscape. The first is managing expectations and their approach per the six factors discussed above. The specialist mode demands an internal incentive system, promotion rules, and an organizational culture that values capability development. In contrast, an organization active in the community mode must build relationships with a large, distributed community, through both monetary and non-monetary incentive mechanisms. This in turn has consequences for the internal culture, which needs to be open-minded to input and suggestions from outside the company; it must not exhibit a "not-invented-here" syndrome. In short, you must create an alignment between your internal structures and the external innovation modes in which you engage.

The next consideration is cultivating new modes for exploration. For example, established firms can benefit from learning how to operate in the venture mode. Today, for many firms, innovation efforts start and stop at innovation spaces and granting "free" time for people to work on personal projects. However, to truly develop an internal venture culture, substantial effort needs to be put into developing a systematic process of coaching, mentoring, internal funding, and executive support – and to have this effort supported over a long period and not just be a corporate initiative of the month. An example of a highly successful program was developed at EMC (now Dell-EMC), a specialist cloud-based information technology company that has spent nearly a decade combining internal communities, networks, and makers through their "Innovation Network." Internal competitions are held annually, with winners tasked with creating their innovations. The effort, supported by upper-level management, encourages employees to become corporate entrepreneurs. Thus far, these efforts have created over $400 million in new business for EMC. Their Innovation Network program has spanned 176 challenges and generated over 17,000 innovation ideas.

Becoming a Multimode Organization

In the past, most companies were active only in a single mode, the precursor of the specialist mode (e.g., Apple in the 1980s and 1990s). In fact, this innovation mode was part of their identity. It described the companies' ambitions to be a leader in high quality, low cost, or some other dimension. As a result, all internal processes were aligned to achieve this goal. Firms aiming to be a low-cost leader reduced variety, increased volume, and invested resources to develop innovations that would support that goal. Ford Motor Company is a classic historical example, with their focus on standardization and eventual cost reduction in the production of the Model T. Dell is a more recent example. For others in the specialist mode, the desire has been to push the boundaries of their efforts, to produce products and services that have features, profit margins, and sales beyond that of their competition.

A multimode organization is one in which the firm has the organizational capability and flexibility to leverage each of the innovation modes when and where needed. This may be to augment their established specialist mode; for example, to include user input in the innovation process via engaged communities on social networks, or to empower individual employees to be makers and begin internal ventures. As we discussed at the beginning of this book, the goal of any innovation process is to have the most good ideas make it to development, to develop them efficiently, and to have them be of high quality and successful in the marketplace. Multimode operation is a way to achieve this.

Playing in multiple modes simultaneously is especially relevant for larger organizations that might leverage different modes in different business units as they look to reconfigure themselves for the challenges of the next decade. General Electric is an example of a

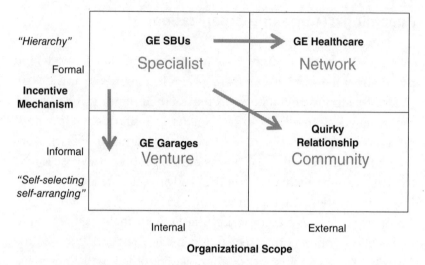

Figure 3.8: GE's activities in the innovation mode framework.
© 2018 Tucker J. Marion, Sebastian K. Fixson.

company that has experimented with modes such as the community mode in its relationship with Quirky and the venture mode in its GE Garages efforts.[9] See Figure 3.8 to see how GE has played in multiple modes with different initiatives. Note their historical experiments with Quirky in the community mode.

Firms need to decide and define when and where to engage in different innovation modes. For example, communities can be the source of insight on new product features or ideas at the front-end, while the network mode can be valuable during complex engineering and design projects. There are several examples of firms beginning to explore these approaches. We previously mentioned GE, which experimented with Quirky and the community mode. Our research has indicated that mode pairings can be a way for organizations to become comfortable with mode exploration. For example, many recent examples pair a specialist with a community (e.g., GE and Quirky, NASA and its software development community). Others such as Autodesk are exploring the network mode, opening large-scale makerspaces in San Francisco and Boston to establish relationships with local universities and startups. These pairings can be explorative, seeking new ideas in the problem space, or specifically targeted to accomplish a task, such as providing a specific engineering solution.

In this chapter, we explored each mode of the expanded innovation landscape. The fact of the matter is that currently, most firms are one-dimensional in their mode of innovation, and few firms are ambidextrous in their approaches. We expand the definition of ambidexterity to include a firm's ability to simultaneously explore multiple modes of innovation concomitantly. This will be explored in more detail in chapter 7.

Summary

The expanded innovation landscape offers firms fresh ways to approach innovation, engage participants in new ways, and develop skills to better leverage the benefits of digital design and collaborative technologies. The real benefit to firms and executives is understanding each of the modes and how they might engage in each one. In the next several chapters, we will explore each mode in greater detail and provide actionable tools and strategies to help companies implement innovation initiatives in each of the modes.

Key Points

• The "perfect storm" of digital design and a collaborative, sharing culture has changed the landscape of innovation.

- Higher levels or performance and lower barriers to entry, as well as more distributed and trust-based collaboration, have created an expanded innovation landscape.
- Four main ways to innovate have emerged in this new digital era: the specialist, venture, community, and network modes.
- Each mode has its own unique "DNA," which leads to opportunities and challenges as firms look to try new modes.
- There are six critical factors that firms should consider when exploring new modes, ranging from resource control to organizational design to incentives.
- Modes are dynamic, and firms can progress to becoming active in multiple modes, increasing the potential for more sources of innovation, higher-quality ideas, and lower costs.

Assessments

Before assessing other modes of innovation new to your firm, you need to understand your current operating condition. To do this, you must investigate several dimensions that are important variables for whether your organization is up to the challenge of exploring new modes and ultimately embracing multimode operation. Think through these variables and assess areas that need improvement. Please use the following questions to assess your current mode.

Collaborative Culture
- Does your organization actively promote a collaborative culture internally and externally?
- Do you use the latest in collaborative tools and information technology?
- Do you promote interaction and engage with communities outside the firm?
- Do you actively pursue open innovation efforts?

Entrepreneurial Mindset
- Do you actively promote and empower employees to develop ideas and projects in an entrepreneurial fashion?
- Do you have a defined, systematic way for employees to develop, pitch, and receive funding for new ideas?
- Do you incentivize entrepreneurial activities?
- Do you measure bottom-up idea generation and project success?
- Does your firm tolerate risk and longer-term strategies?

Performance Orientation
- Are you considered a market leader in your industry segment?
- Do you push boundaries of product/service performance and business model innovation?
- Do you implement leading-edge technologies and manufacturing techniques into current and future products/services?
- Is intellectual property essential in innovation efforts?

Network Maturity
- Do you rely on outside suppliers and vendors to partner with for your innovation efforts?
- Are new-to-the-world products and services jointly developed with partners?
- Are critical innovation and design tasks done outside the corporation?
- Are R&D teams empowered to freely explore outside collaborations and relationships to improve the innovation process?

The Specialist Mode

In the last chapter we discussed the expanded innovation landscape and the formation of new modes of innovation. The intersection of digital design and a collaborative culture certainly has enabled open innovation and spurred the maker movement. But the perfect storm is no less impactful to the *specialists*. The specialist mode comprises high-performance market-segment leaders that fully leverage the benefits of digital design and collaborative technology. Porsche, NASA, SpaceX, Boeing, McLaren, and the design firm IDEO are all examples of organizations that push the boundaries of how digital design can be integrated into the innovation process.

What we see is an opportunity for specialists to reinvent their culture and process, leveraging these technologies to their fullest. Firms need to think of this as their "moonshot" opportunity – to leapfrog their competitors by getting to the bleeding edge of design and interaction. However, just purchasing 3D printers and fostering video calls among team members is not the recipe for success. The transformative nature comes from how you use these technologies and what you do with them. Simply put, the specialist mode affords new, extreme levels of product performance, new approaches to operations, service, and customer interaction, and the development of new business models.

Almost all traditional firms after founding and growth become rooted in the specialist mode. These firms deal with common issues surrounding innovation such as intense global competition, the specter of disruption, changes in technology, or the fickle nature of consumer preferences. The aim of this chapter is to discuss how you can break out of the pack by transforming your firm into a digital design and collaboration powerhouse.

Firms like GE have invested heavily in the digital transformation. And while as of this writing GE is dealing with difficult challenges, the amount of effort they put into digital design and collaborative efforts is impressive. GE boasts that it has over 300 3D printers currently in use (and is on its way to over 1,000), and these are involved in cutting, painting, and fabricating parts used in critical systems such as jet engines. GE estimates it will have manufactured approximately 100,000 additive-manufactured parts for aerospace applications by 2020.[1] In 2016, GE invested over $1 billion to acquire European 3D-printing firms Arcam and SLM Solutions. However, their embrace of these technologies goes well beyond buying a 3D printer for R&D. Instead, the organization embraces this technology at all levels, including management in science and R&D, business development, and operations. GE sees itself as one of the companies that will hit new levels of growth and market expansion using the technology, and as such this thinking permeates the organization in a much deeper way than new technology use alone. Consider, for example, a manufacturing facility for jet aircraft engines in New Hampshire, where 3D printers in the tool room have changed the way jigs and gauges for production assembly are made and used. An engineer on the shop floor (who wished to remain anonymous) explained to us: "3D printing has really changed the way we approach things. It's almost like having another skilled person in the tool shop. It gives us extra capacity and allows us to design new types of tools and make them faster. And these tools have other side benefits, making the tools lighter and safer for the assembler. We can also create new shapes that can be stored vertically, saving shop floor space. Now the culture has changed: we always ask first if a tool can be 3D printed. And now skilled labor is not skeptical, but sees it as a valuable tool, allowing them to spend more time on higher-skilled projects." Former GE CEO Jeff Immelt noted that in transforming the company by using these technologies, "we want to be one of the companies that does that." Since 2010, GE has invested about $1.5 billion in additive manufacturing.[2] While the return on this investment may not be immediate, as shown by turmoil in GE's management team and stock price as this book was being written, the turning of an industrial giant to this realm is a necessity. A former GE sales executive noted, "The push to digital and additive manufacturing is the right thing to do. Ultimately they will be a stronger company in five years because of it."[3] The effective embrace of digital transformation by individual business units such as aerospace creates a platform for increased value in the future, regardless of current uncertainties of the organization as a whole.

The pace of innovation in additive manufacturing keeps accelerating, giving specialists even greater ability to innovate in design and process. The MIT spin-out Desktop Metal is commercializing a new metal printing technology that can print structural parts much more efficiently than current processes. Co-founder Professor John Hart notes that this technology can lead to "customized mass production."[4]

Specialists are using digital design and collaboration to change not only how they develop new products but also their business model itself. Let's look at the Canadian medical device company

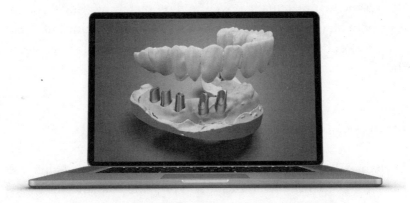

Figure 4.1: Dental Wings' imaging and design tools for dental implants. Photo courtesy of Dental Wings.

Dental Wings. Dental Wings (www.dentalwings.com) is a provider of digital dentistry technologies, from new in-mouth scanning technologies to 3D-printed tools to help improve the accuracy of outcomes for dental implants and dentures. What makes Dental Wings such a good example is not just that they are improving patient care and outcomes – that is for sure all-important. It is that they are pushing the envelope of digital technology to improve the patient/doctor experience, while simultaneously adding new business models and services that were not possible before the digital perfect storm. Their scanning technology, use of additive manufacturing, and development of an enhanced network to help improve the process is exactly the kind of virtuous cycle that fully embracing digital design and collaborative initiatives can bring to firms. Another example is the automotive start-up Divergent (www.divergent3d.com). Divergent is creating next-generation 3D-printing technology that it sees as a technology platform to automate the design and manufacture of automobiles. They are designing not only the car, but the tools that can design and manufacture it as well, and ultimately offering this technology to others.[5] In the next section, we discuss key attributes and examples of how to become a leading-edge specialist by leveraging the two forces.

Embracing the Tools and Changing the Culture

In chapter 2, we described the perfect storm of forces combining to expand the innovation landscape. On one side you have the digitization of the design process, from hyper-capable design software to increasingly sophisticated additive-manufacturing techniques. On the other side, you have the emergence of a highly collaborative, sharing culture enabled at least in part by information technology.

The proliferation of these new ways to design and share information among R&D teams has been pervasive. In nearly every aspect of the life cycle of an innovation project, new tools have been developed. From brainstorming tools like Stormboard to file-sharing with Dropbox, to project wikis like Basecamp, leading specialists have embraced these. And the best-performing specialists use these tools much more frequently than those that do not.

Recent research on over 400 global firms, ranging from small businesses to the largest of multinational corporations, indicates that the best-performing firms (as measured by new product development performance as defined by time-to-market, performance to specifications, and budget performance) use these tools much more frequently than poorer performing firms. And though the overall usage of these collaborative tools is relatively low among the total sample of firms, when firms do use them intensely, their influence on project performance is strong. This indicates that firms should look to adopt these tools and increase their usage during all phases of the NPD process.[6]

Specialists leading the way, like SpaceX, are early and heavy adopters of these new technologies. They integrate digital design and additive manufacturing into their innovation process intensively while simultaneously experimenting with new forms of sharing, information exchange, and collaboration. Here are some examples of firms maximizing their use of both digital design and collaborative tools while simultaneously integrating them into their culture and approach to innovation.

ACEINNA, Inc. – Digital Design Changing Customer Development and Interaction

ACEINNA, Inc. (www.aceinna.com), headquartered in Andover, Massachusetts, is a world leader in micromechanical sensors, having recently shipped its billionth accelerometer. They produce sensors and systems that play critical roles in automotive, aerospace, and consumer products.

In terms of digital design, ACEINNA uses virtual design and simulation extensively. From gas flow simulations to advanced algorithm testing, ACEINNA invests substantial effort into design verification throughout the conceptualization and design process. In addition, they 3D-print concepts continually for quick team design review cycles. An even more important change to the innovation process is the use of 3D-printed parts during the business development process. ACEINNA uses 3D printing to quickly put evaluation parts in the hands of potential customers. This has a number of benefits. First, this speeds up the customer evaluation and iteration process greatly. The development and iterative cycles for design and requirements can occur with customers in real time, in essence giving companies that produce physical products a very agile, software-development-like integration of customers and quick validation. Second, the process of early prototyping and customer development is a boon for business and relationship development. For ACEINNA, this allowed them to move from having no involvement in certain industry verticals to having real partnerships in brand-new applications like the internet of things (IoT). Since 3D-printed parts such as those from stereo-lithography have near production-like tolerance and strength properties for plastic parts, the earlier original equipment manufacturer (OEM) firms can design their parts from suppliers like ACEINNA, the more predictable future business with new partners can be. For collaboration tools, ACEINNA uses a suite of collaborative project tools like Basecamp, Teamwork.com, and Skype for business. Because their business is split between China and the United States, cloud-based collaboration software is key to maintaining progress during R&D.[7]

Continuum Innovation – Collaborative Technology and Modified Culture Enhancing the Process

Continuum (www.continuuminnovation.com) is a global innovation design firm, headquartered in Boston. To increase performance among the team for their client projects, they designed their new office space to accommodate their collaborative workstyle. No longer do project managers have desks; they "float" among the design team and have no permanent home. To foster communication with other offices (like Shanghai, China, for example), a wall-sized projector and constant-on Skype connection has been established. This office "window" has become a real asset in managing projects between global studios. As for digital design, Continuum maintains a suite of on-site 3D printers and CNC (computer numerically controlled) milling machines to quickly manufacture and assemble looks-like and functional prototypes.

In fact, the centerpiece of their new office space (shown in Figure 4.2) in the Innovation District in Boston is an internal

Figure 4.2: Collaboration and Made Real prototyping space at Continuum's new office space in Boston, MA. Photo courtesy of Continuum.

prototype space that has the entire spectrum of digital design tools available to the engineers and designers at all times, called the Made Real Lab. All these factors combine to allow Continuum's client project teams to be extremely effective and fast. This has allowed Continuum not only to produce award-winning designs but to marry that to exceptionally complex engineering.

SpaceX – Digital Design Transforming the Development-to-Manufacturing Process

SpaceX has fully embraced digital design, including developing internally sourced custom solutions that change the way you interact with their digital models of rockets and capsules. They have experimented with a combination of hand gesture controls to manipulate parts on a virtual reality display. For CAD, SpaceX uses Siemens NX software. This advanced software handles all design efforts for their Falcon rockets and Dragon space capsule.

This CAD software suite is also used on the manufacturing floor, to check design and assembly in real time. SpaceX estimates a 50 percent productivity improvement using these new CAD suites and collaborative software.[8] In addition, SpaceX uses additive manufacturing to improve the performance and lower the cost of some of their rocket nozzles. According to 3DPrint.com, "By using such innovative technology ... they [SpaceX] are able to fabricate components like the thrusters with extremely strong and durable 3D printing material – at a fraction of the cost, and in much less time."[9]

PTC – Internal Experimentation Leading to New Product Features

PTC is a global software company that delivers a technology platform and solutions to help companies design, manufacture, operate, and service products for a smart, connected world. From CAD software to product lifecycle management (PLM) software to IoT and augmented reality (AR), PTC software and systems touch nearly every aspect of the innovation process. In an interview with executives in their advanced technology council, they highlighted their experiment on the use (and potential benefit) of new tools and collaborative technologies. These included software from very new firms, firms that would not have passed the approval process of the central IT organization in the past. The teams, empowered to try new things, would evaluate the potential benefit to NPD workflow, in addition to seeing where new technology could enhance their current suite of enterprise software. Their experiments internally with Yammer and Twitter led them to look to integrate social media functionality into their array of NPD tools, specifically in CREO, their 3D CAD suite.

Enhancing the Specialist Mode

So what do you do that's different? How do you change the organization to fully leverage these new technologies and integrate them into the culture? Every company uses CAD and the latest software tools and tries new apps to communicate. The "secret sauce" in getting to the front of the digital and collaborative transformation is considering the foundations framework described in chapter 3. These have ramifications for the design of the organization, its culture, how talent is handled, and how resources are deployed.

Level 1: Mode Foundations

Resource Control
Successful specialists have strong control over their resources, be they internal or external. But control doesn't need to be autocratic, like Yahoo!'s former CEO Marissa Meyer's stipulation of in-person face time at the office. Rather, it's a close understanding of who is doing what, how many resources are being spent, and who is held accountable.

For example, Alan Mulally, early in his tenure at Ford, instituted a "traffic light" reporting system to track new vehicle development. At first, his direct reports were showing a sea of green, with a little yellow sprinkled in (green means all project items are good, red the opposite). Mulally, in a soft yet strong demeanor, indicated that this could not be possible. The next week, according to reports, lots of red showed at the Thursday meeting.[10] From that point forward, the CEO knew exactly where projects stood, and all levels were accountable. Under Mulally's guidance, Ford returned to profitability and growth after years of steady decline. This is a simple yet powerful anecdote of how resources can be managed in a manner that is serious, dignified, and empowering for the innovation team. This is very different from the environment at some other companies.

Intellectual Property

Intellectual property development, protection, and strategy are the bedrock of the specialists. And while firms like Tesla have made their IP open to foster market development, the traditional view of the importance of IP remains a foundation of the high-performing specialist. Look no further than the fight between Apple and Samsung on patent infringement. In 2012, Apple was awarded $1 billion in damages (which was ultimately scaled down to about $500 million). In another case, Apple won a $120 million lawsuit for damages for the infringement of smartphone design. In early 2016, Samsung won an appeal, which relieves Samsung from payment.[11] Regardless of the victor in these cases, the importance of IP for these global companies is all-important. Specialists need to consider IP strategy as a core facet of their innovation process.

However, as we will see in chapters 5 and 6, the new community and network modes of development are shifting firms' views of IP. Both Tesla and SpaceX have given public access to their IP portfolios. In the case of SpaceX and their Hyperloop concept, this is designed to spur innovation and develop the technology. Other firms, such as Redhat, base their business on open-source software. So there is an argument to be made that in very new and innovative industries, closed IP may be a hindrance to market development. Kodak had a lot of IP on digital photography and related technology but was unable to truly capitalize on that protected knowledge.

To sum, IP strategy is important to the specialist and needs to be an integral consideration when deciding how teams approach and leverage innovation. While tightly controlled IP is important, you need to be open to other strategies, as we have seen with firms that have opened their portfolio, like Tesla.

Level 2: Organizational Development

Organizational Design

Large corporations tend to manage their resources in a traditional manner. This means matrix-based organizations where individuals involved in R&D work on multiple projects. Efficient? Yes. The best practice for innovation? Perhaps not. In a study of new ventures, the organization and their approach were investigated to see the differences these successful start-ups had over traditional firms. The research found that start-ups, regardless of industry, have small, hyper-agile teams that can freely move about and source what they need when they need it. The best specialists give their innovation teams this ability to be a new venture within the corporate walls and have them work in their own mode. And this is not a Lockheed Martin–type Skunk Works with teams separated from the organization. It's an open and empowered approach to self-management and government, supported by the C-suite.[12] We'll discuss these corporate ventures in much more detail in chapter 4.

Organizational design goes beyond team structure to address management hierarchy, office design, and the culture itself. Look no further than design firms like IDEO and Continuum. These highly innovative project teams are staffed with people with varied backgrounds, project management can rotate during the project, and the projects are run with a process that eschews onerous procedures like rigorous stage gates. These look a little different from your typical Fortune 500 firm.[13] For your next innovative project, look to these specialists as inspiration as you develop a highly capable and empowered hyper-agile team.

Task Allocation

For specialists, highly skilled R&D teams are a major asset. These firms need to attract the best talent and have them be hyper-productive. In fact, recent articles have noted that it's harder to get a job at a firm like Alphabet (Google's parent company) than it is to get into Harvard.[14] According to Staff.com, only 1 out of 130 applicants gets a job. However, once there, these employees earn high salaries, enjoy generous perks, and are presented with a host of opportunities. The challenge for firms is to have a culture that is supportive and empowering and enables a work-life balance. These internal resources are invaluable for the continued innovation of these firms.

Without this talent, the next Porsche model or the newest virtual reality headset simply won't get realized in the right form in the right time. Internal talent needs nurturing and development. Look at a firm like EMC (now Dell-EMC). Their culture embraces continued education and development. From technical training to generous tuition reimbursement, EMC believes that enrichment is key. In fact, every EMC employee received $50,000 in lifetime learning resources to enable them to earn higher-level degrees. EMC even brought local universities in-house for custom, sponsored MBA programs. Cultivating top talent and keeping them energized, well-trained, and valued is all-important. If firms do not accomplish this, another specialist will be there to poach employees. As mentioned in chapter 2, look no further than the back and forth of cross-town hiring between Apple and Tesla. Tesla's poaching bonus for former Apple employees in 2015 was $250,000 and a 60 percent increase in salary![15]

You have a talented team, but they are not co-located like Apple's Project Titan (their code name for the rumored Apple car). Like most companies, yours is probably multinational, with business units and R&D that stretch globally. How important is collaboration?

It is very important, as connections between these disparate R&D resources are essential. Increased connections equal increased effectiveness. And in light of the decentralization and globalization of work processes, most firms have responded to their dynamic environments by introducing virtual teams, in which members are geographically dispersed and coordinate their work mainly through information and communication technologies.[16] Think Zoom, Apple FaceTime, and Google Chat. Teams need to embrace these as a fundamental work habit to increase communication frequency and effectiveness. As managers, you also need to give your teams the ability to try new communication tools and play with them. The 23-year-old on the development team may just have the right new communication app (e.g., the latest Snap, previously Snapchat) or latest project management tool (e.g., the Slack of tomorrow no one has heard of yet). This could transform the team and its performance.

In tying this together, a talented team, whether co-located or internationally distributed, needs to have the latest tools to function properly. Knowledge management is all-important, or else information falls through the gaps and teams don't function as well. This is all driven by software, infrastructure, and the approach taken toward them.[17] The companies that do this well function extremely well in leveraging global assets for innovation. A recent study showed that firms' shared knowledge with suppliers and developing country subsidiaries is a key attribute in developing their innovation assets, both in incremental and more radical innovations.[18]

Empowered hyper-functional team? Check. Latest design and communication tools? Check. Key IP and performance objectives developed? Check. Now you have to implement and execute. Tasks need to be allocated and managed. Who does what? Do you insource or outsource? This is where the empowered team needs to be given the authority to autonomously make decisions. An example is the original General Motors (GM) Chevrolet Volt project, which *Wired* magazine dubbed a moonshot.[19] After the initial idea, the company developed a small team, which included resources spanning the entire company and eventually included key suppliers like LG Chemical. The team was given a clear goal: to create the best green car in the world – the world's first extended-range electric vehicle (EV). Decision-making authority was given to the team, and traditional gates/decision points and bureaucracy were removed.[20] The project was developed and commercialized in an incredibly short period of time for such a complex vehicle (arguably the most complex vehicle in the world when introduced in late 2010). Team responsibilities were clear, but as in a start-up, all team members wore "many hats" and were committed to getting the job done. Give your teams this ability; it is essential. The Volt was the *Motor Trend* Car of the Year in 2011 and helped GM push to the forefront of EV technology.

Level 3: Implementation

Incentives

In this chapter we discussed the importance of empowered teams. So how do you motivate them? We know from research that monetary compensation is not as highly a rated motivator as many think. Specialists succeeding at innovation offer other incentives, giving time and recognition for innovative efforts. While Silicon Valley provides food, limitless vacation, and on-site dry cleaning, these may be just perks for happy workers. To foster innovation in a deep sense from the bottom up, the best specialists give their teams ownership over their destiny. Think of the original Apple Macintosh team: they had their own flag – a pirate flag that was flown over their offices in Cupertino and stenciled on T-shirts!

New KPIs

Moving beyond the basics like return on investment (ROI) to longer-term goals, other new KPIs like true business model innovation, sustainability, and societal impact are increasingly important. Highly effective specialists have added new KPIs to help innovation teams push boundaries and expand their scope. Here are some important KPIs that move beyond the basics:

- Does the new innovation project enhance or change the firm's business model?
- Does it add new, profound ways to touch the customer?
- Does the innovation project include new services?
- Does it allow interaction with the customer throughout the product life cycle?
- Can the product or service be enhanced during its life cycle?
- Is the innovation socially and environmentally responsible?

Summary

To be the most effective specialist, there are a few main points to consider. The first is that as a department, strategic business unit (SBU), or firm, you need to fully embrace the potential of digital design and collaboration. But embracing does not mean just purchasing a few high-end 3D printers and using Slack. No, it is an immersion into exploring the capabilities of these two forces and challenging your teams to push the envelope – not only of product performance but also of how the technology can transform business and service models and where and how you touch your customers. To do this, you need to work through the Six Factors and begin to change the organization, embedding these two forces in the culture from the bottom up (not just the top down).

Key Points

- Specialists are embracing the two forces and using the inherent advantages in the technology not only to affect design performance but also to create new process and business models.
- Embracing digital design and a collaborative culture in an intense fashion is allowing firms to iterate faster and challenge the status quo in performance.
- Specialists are using these tools to develop more mature conceptual designs, in many cases getting them into the field to test and validate new opportunities while cultivating new relationships.
- Leading firms are in some cases creating their own technologies. Or they are allowing their teams to use tools (design and collaboration) from small new ventures. Experimentation is a hallmark of leading specialists.
- Retaining talent and offering appropriate incentives play a crucial role, as the talent pool is a constraint, which may get worse in coming years.

Assessments

To assist you in bringing your specialist teams to the next level, here are some key questions you need to honestly ask yourself and your team. Rate your organization on a scale of 1 to 5 (1 being "not at all" and 5 being "extensively"). Generally, lower scores suggest an opportunity to embrace both digital design and a sharing, collaborative culture more fully within your innovation process.

Design and Collaborative Culture
- Does your organization actively promote a collaborative culture internally and externally?

- Do you use the latest in collaborative tools and information technology?
- Do you use additive manufacturing (3D printing) in commercialized products?
- Do you allow teams to make their own decisions about tool use?

Performance Orientation
- Are you considered a market leader in your industry segment?
- Do you push boundaries of product/service performance and business model innovation?
- Do you implement leading-edge technologies and manufacturing techniques into current and future products/services?
- Is intellectual property essential in your innovation efforts?

Where are you the weakest? Focus on these areas first. Ideally, you should be highly rated in each category. It will take time and effort to get there though. Also, these two main topics have relevance for the other modes in the coming chapters. Expertise in these areas will help as you seek to develop other innovation modes.

The Venture Mode

In the previous chapter we presented the specialist mode as a mode in which digital design enables previously unseen levels of high-performance product and service solutions. But the rapid development in digital design tools, together with the emergence of a collaborative culture, also has another effect that causes the innovation landscape to expand. The effect is that the decrease in price and the increase in usability of digital design tools have drastically lowered the barrier of entry. As a result, a rising number of new players have entered the competition, both individual inventors and innovators within the walls of existing firms. For established companies, we can draw tangible lessons from these ventures and their approaches to leveraging the benefits of digital design and collaborative culture.

In chapter 3 we introduced the start-up U-Turn, who through the use of many digital design tools – many of them web-based, some of them even free – managed to knit together a system of design and production resources to quickly build prototypes and test market demand. Although the title of this chapter may remind many of new firms, as an innovation mode, the venture mode focuses on small units that can move fast within companies. These can exist as independent start-ups or as units internally within larger organizations or business units. What makes this mode unique is that the ease of use and abundance of low- or no-cost resources enable fast and inexpensive development of concepts and testable prototypes. This can dramatically increase the number of potential opportunities a firm, or an individual entrepreneur, can explore.

An important characteristic in both settings is that the dominant coordination mechanism is not direct control through hierarchy – as in the specialist mode – but rather a form of self-selection and repeated pruning through market forces as new information emerges. And because it is quick and inexpensive, you can do a lot more exploration. To understand the value of more exploration, let's turn our lens to the perspective of venture capitalists (VCs) in the start-up world. VCs vet each investment through the due diligence process, but overall the expectation is that only one or two out of 10 investments pay off. In other words, collectively the investments are a set of bets because of the unknowability of future performance. For firms, the venture mode allows more bets, just as lower-cost, lean start-ups and their minimally viable products (MVPs) have enabled a greater number of smaller-equity financing rounds.

Let's add a little more entrepreneurial context. The large and rapid capital expenditures seen at firms like the start-up Webvan (nearly $1 billion spent in funding[1]) in the late 1990s have been replaced by a much more pragmatic and results-driven development process and culture. This is epitomized by the propagation of lean start-up methodologies.[2] While every framework and methodology has its limitations, the concepts of evidence-based entrepreneurship, the minimally viable functional prototype, and continuous learning are extremely powerful and valuable. New ventures are driven to shorter development cycles and to fail faster in their learning process. It seems to have worked for these start-ups, and it works in the context of larger firms that allow their employees to explore the venture mode.

Thanks to the advances in digital design, today it costs less and there are more resources available to develop your project from the zero-stage. Developing an internet start-up in the 1990s required you to develop your own infrastructure, which was capital intensive from both a human and a financial resource perspective. There were no Amazon web services for hosting, or tool kits like Invision[3] to help develop wireframe mock-ups for demonstrating mobile app features for almost no cost. Physical rapid prototypes were the bastion of large firms, and freelance industrial designers were not a click away. Today, these new technologies and services have enabled an expansive cadre of outsourced capabilities beneficial to the early-stage venture.[4] During the 1990s technology boom, there were incubators but certainly not the depth and breadth of resources available to today's entrepreneurs. From MassChallenge, a not-for-profit accelerator creating global movement to support entrepreneurship,[5] to higher-education-centric groups, like the student-run IDEA venture accelerator at Northeastern University,[6] this ecosystem of support allows new ventures to move much faster, much farther, with fewer of the venture's own resources. A relatively small seed investment can enable a team to develop a functional prototype of a new mobile application, validate its business model, gather user data, and develop relationships with strategic partners – setting itself up for a larger investment, assuming it meets the required milestones. Simply stated, you get more for your seed money today than you did in 1997. And the playing field is more varied, from food innovation to IoT applications. The Dormroomfund is an example of structured equity finance that goes to a greater number of smaller investments.[7] The Dormroomfund brings together student entrepreneurs and student investors, who make investments of up to

$20,000. Additional services, networking, and mentoring are also provided to the teams. Crowdfunding sites like Kickstarter and Indiegogo have provided further sources of funding to the budding entrepreneur.

The same spirit of more, lower-cost yet riskier investments that angel groups and early-stage VCs now leverage can also be fostered inside a large organization. This allows a firm to have many more ideas being considered at the beginning of the innovation funnel. With more seeds, the chances of better innovations coming out improve significantly. Consider the innovation system that EMC built over the past decade.[8] In 2008, the then CTO (chief technology officer) created a company-wide innovation contest to which over 400 employees submitted ideas. Thirty of these ideas were selected as finalists, and three of those were publicly celebrated as contest winners. EMC learned, however, that while the innovation contest was very successful in generating a pool of ideas, in itself it was not enough for an idea to become a commercial product.

Over the years, EMC adjusted and tweaked its process to increase the alignment between the strategic needs of the major business units and the idea pool generated company-wide by the employees. For example, business units began to put forward challenges into which employees with relevant ideas self-selected. In addition, EMC created an incubation process that supported the winning ideas to develop into commercial products. This process, called the Innovation Network, provided educational content, active learning, and mentoring to these internal new ventures as they progressed through milestones. Ultimately projects are presented to management to vie for seed funding. Internal estimates note that the Innovation Network has contributed approximately $400 million in new revenue.

In another example, at a large pharmaceutical company in 2014, select individuals from across the development organization were chosen to go through an innovation boot camp and internal venturing process. After a period of two months of concept refinement, projects were presented to an internal "VC" panel. Two of three teams were ultimately given seed funding of approximately $150,000. Team contributors could leave their current assignments to be on the team full-time and see the projects go through prototyping, testing, and validation. Both projects were successfully implemented and are currently being rolled out to the organization.

In another example, at GE Appliances, the head of R&D lamented that a novel way of making ice cubes sat on the shelf for 20 years. Through their FirstBuild[9] initiative, they were able to quickly develop a product concept and upload it to the crowdfunding site Indiegogo. The concept, Opal, raised $2.7 million in 2015.[10] What makes Indiegogo so relevant to the venture mode is that it is a way to gain and validate customer feedback. The potential customers are voting with their wallets. And it gives the venture team funds to develop their innovation. Indiegogo estimates using their platform can reduce time-to-market by months, all the while getting invaluable feedback from potential customers. Firms from Hasbro to Whirlpool are using the Indiegogo platform as an integral part of the venture mode to validate their innovation concepts.

A key factor enabling these venture project efforts are the number of service providers that have emerged who provide this type of support to independent start-ups. Via the internet, start-ups can now find easily providers that offer services ranging from software for design, testing, and a wide array of analyses to prototype manufacturing through 3D-printing services, inventory, and fulfillment services. In this marketplace of ideas, entire supply chains can be quickly built and reconfigured as needed. In the venture mode, the central theme is providing resources that can enable fast development and a validation cycle for the self-starting individual or small team. In the next section, we review how the Six Factors influence and shape this mode.

Level 1: Mode Foundations

Resource Control

There are a number of factors to consider. The first is the start-up team itself in how it controls the resources it needs. It may be as simple as a transaction of purchasing services. This then is a matter of assembling the right resources and coordinating and controlling them. Quick assembly and configuration are key. Consider U-Turn: their ability to source key components locally through 100kgarages.com, leverage micro investment from a university, and test their MVP using 3D-printed parts sourced through rapid prototyping service provider Quickparts (now part of 3D Systems) enabled extremely quick response and validation with potential customers. The founders' success boiled down to using the right vendors and being effective project managers. For the venture within an existing corporation, a challenge can be giving the team the authority to use services outside and inside the firm with little or no oversight from purchasing departments, onerous budget procedures, and so forth. In fact, in our investigations of successful new ventures, the most successful firms eschewed traditional processes like stage gates and traditional approaches to marketing, instead establishing a culture in which milestones were key. Progress was valued much more heavily than process.[11] For your venture mode efforts, remove red tape, bureaucracy, and procedures.[12] As one entrepreneur noted in the research, "We did what we had to do to get the job done."[13] That, in essence, is the entrepreneurial spirit that ventures in existing firms need to capture. And it starts with control – letting them be real ventures in control of their own destiny.

Intellectual Property

While in each of the modes IP is a concern, the venture mode has unique challenges and opportunities. Because the teams in this mode are internal, the firm remains in control. This can result in an approach to IP that is not unlike the approaches taken in the specialist mode. However, the big benefit of this mode is the possibility of lots of ideas being generated, more being prototyped and "kicked around," and several being selected for rapid development. IP should not slow this process down, as one of the main advantages of the venture mode is speed. This may mean a higher reliance on more general provisional applications; rather than starting the rigorous process of utility patents early, delay them. Whereas a more liberal IP approach may be riskier in terms of the competition, the competitive advantage of speed often trumps it.

Level 2: Organizational Development

Organizational Design

Setting up idea hunts and having winning teams is the easy part. The hard part is establishing an ingrained innovation ecosystem that funds, mentors, empowers, and rewards individuals and teams for these efforts over the long term. Several factors are at play in the organizational design. The first is space itself, which is now becoming ubiquitous in the firms we researched. Central innovation labs, internal maker spaces, and communal spaces today are what the cubicle was to the 1970s. However, building an innovation space and hoping the new ideas come is a sure-fire way for the effort to run a short course and have it fall into the boneyard of failed corporate initiatives.[14] In a Boston-area large medical device firm, the new innovation lab we visited was empty. Its celebration balloons collected dust on the floor.

However, physical space is important. From the work of Thomas Allen in the 1970s on workspace communication and collaboration to the design of Apple's new Cupertino, California, headquarters, we know that the layout and fostering of interaction is tied to communication, collaboration, knowledge flow, and ultimately innovation success.[15] Apple's new circular headquarters is intentionally designed to foster this informal communication and interaction. The outer rings are designed to promote cross-pollination of employees, while the large central spaces are communal spaces for meeting and working.

In looking at improving spaces and collaboration, you need to consider the larger context. Location, design, access, and integration into the larger culture are important. In chapter 4 we discussed the innovation design firm Continuum. Their new offices contain open and reconfigurable common spaces and conference rooms; this multi-use aspect promotes open communication and collaboration. Their new space is used not only for client projects but also for community outreach and social events.

The second consideration concerns the teams themselves. And here's where we can learn from start-ups. Across industries, we have found the most successful teams exhibit characteristics that allows them to move fast. They are small – five to seven members seems to be the sweet spot – but are multifunctional so that they have the skills necessary to perform any tasks (and can access missing skills quickly). We call these teams *hyper-functional*. Successful teams possess a culture that produces internally what has been called psychological safety (i.e., they create an environment in which team members are not afraid to try out new ideas).[16] Externally, successful teams have enough room to maneuver through experiments, because some of them will fail if the team pushes the envelope in its innovation efforts. In other words, teams need to be empowered to run through fast cycles of iterations to quickly learn what works and what doesn't.

These teams have the ability to move the project forward quickly: doing their own research, iterating and applying rapid development, and getting the project done quickly. But these teams need support, not only from direct managers but from the C-suite as well. In our research we have found that when teams are given moral support, financial support, and direct mentoring, they can be extremely successful. In one of the projects we observed, the project lead was able to test and build a lead user community by using his business unit's unused expense budget. This creative use of unused funds was not typical but was approved by management even though it wasn't standard procedure. What distinguishes this case is that the firm allowed this to happen at all. The easier route would be for management to say no, but this type of flexibility and support is a trait of firms that foster a successful venture mode. And situations like these are attracting global attention. Japanese companies are increasingly trying to foster environments that are more start-up-like.[17] They see this as the key to moving away from their lost decade(s) of decreasing performance and innovation.

The third key aspect is the infrastructure of the process itself. In other words, it is the phased process these ventures use to move the projects along that makes the difference. From a high level, an overall framework consisting of three phases can work well. An example is Northeastern University's IDEA, a new venture creation system that uses a concept of "Ready, Set, Go."[18] At the end of the "Go" phase, new ventures compete for seed investment. But along the way, each venture is supported by mentoring, along with in-kind and micro investment, such as a prototype fund. A schematic of the process is shown in Figure 5.1. And while this is tailored for start-ups, a similar process can be implemented at existing firms to foster the venture mode.

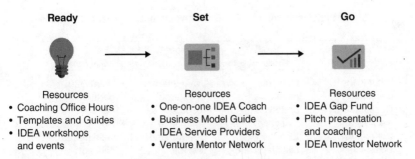

Ready	Set	Go
Resources	Resources	Resources
• Coaching Office Hours	• One-on-one IDEA Coach	• IDEA Gap Fund
• Templates and Guides	• Business Model Guide	• Pitch presentation
• IDEA workshops	• IDEA Service Providers	and coaching
and events	• Venture Mentor Network	• IDEA Investor Network

Figure 5.1: Northeastern's IDEA new venture accelerator stage-gate process. Photo courtesy of Northeastern University.

For companies seeking to develop an integrated venturing eco-system within their own walls, our research and work in executive education suggests a few process-related items that need to be considered. A first step is boot camps. Made up of a cross-section of motivated employees from across the organization, these can start the education process *and* innovative projects simultaneously. A three-day, intense boot camp in corporate entrepreneurship and innovation can start with pressing organizational, product, and service issues that can be distilled into actionable concepts by the end of the session. Next, employees should be given the ability to stay on and complete the projects, at least through the MVP validation process. Along the way, coaching and mentoring need to be completed, along with milestone reviews and seed funding where appropriate. For the teams themselves, the simple framework shown in Figure 5.2 can be used effectively as they go from concept through testing prototypes. We find that the original team should be kept intact and that its core team be a consistent presence throughout the development process. Note that resource allocation is specifically highlighted. This encourages the team to find and use outside resources to speed development. For validation planning, early prototypes can be field-tested, or platforms like Indiegogo can be used effectively.

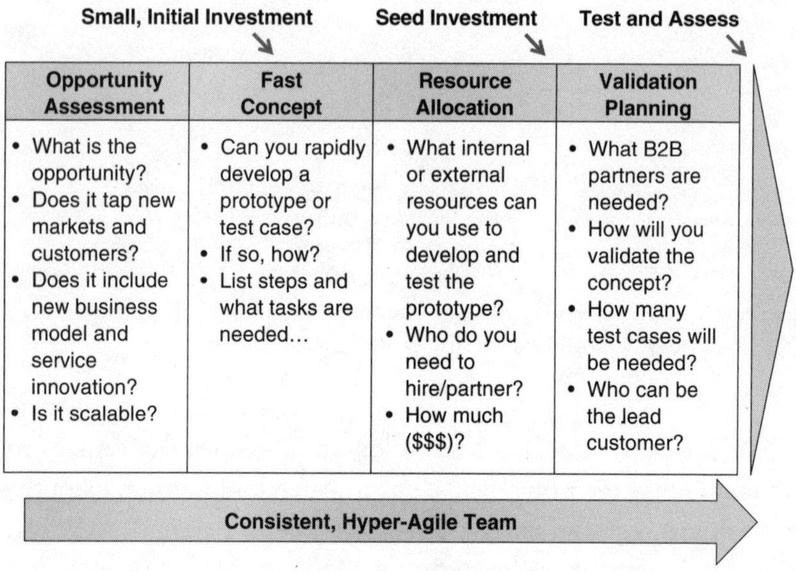

Small, Initial Investment	Seed Investment	Test and Assess	
Opportunity Assessment	**Fast Concept**	**Resource Allocation**	**Validation Planning**
• What is the opportunity? • Does it tap new markets and customers? • Does it include new business model and service innovation? • Is it scalable?	• Can you rapidly develop a prototype or test case? • If so, how? • List steps and what tasks are needed...	• What internal or external resources can you use to develop and test the prototype? • Who do you need to hire/partner? • How much ($$$)?	• What B2B partners are needed? • How will you validate the concept? • How many test cases will be needed? • Who can be the lead customer?

Consistent, Hyper-Agile Team

Figure 5.2: Lean innovation framework for the venture mode.

After the projects are validated through prototyping, an effective pitch should be presented to C-suite managers, with the intent of asking for investment. It is recommended that two to three projects be funded to a limited rollout to test viability.

Next, the venture network needs to be formalized. Coaches, mentors, and an online learning system that provides content and support should be sourced and developed. This provides infrastructure and support to the program as it scales. This is one of the key factors the EMC Innovation Network implemented. Originally, their framework drew from NASA and other organizations before it was enhanced by feedback from participants and managers. Eventually, coaching and training in an online environment was provided for each of the Innovation Network teams. As we have expressed in this chapter, other items now can be added to the effort. These include dedicated innovation spaces, more refined incentives for the teams, and importantly, long-term support from upper-level management.

Task Allocation
In the venture mode the individuals and small teams are drivers of new ideas. However, the commercialization potential of the ideas is not evenly distributed. In other words, some teams work on winning ideas, whereas the ideas of some other teams will turn out to be duds. For managers engaged in this innovation process, that insight translates into three major tasks. First, create an environment in which ideas can emerge in the first place. The theoretical argument for using contests to do so is that they essentially represent a set of parallel experiments, a process that is very fast. In spirit, this is not unlike an idea hunt, in which a firm taps a community of users or customers for input on new products and services. An example is Lays asking its customers for potato chip flavor ideas. The second task in the venture mode is to build an infrastructure that can support the incubation of a smaller number of ideas, including a way to expose them in incremental steps to increasing market forces (such as posting them on crowdfunding sites and getting prototypes into early field testing). This encompasses a defined process to guide the ventures and structure to provide mentoring and education, as we discussed with the lean innovation framework and examples like IDEA. Consideration in developing the infrastructure should also include mechanisms to allow individuals to contribute and be encouraged to participate from upper-level management without affecting day-job performance.

Third, give the team the resources to develop, prototype, learn, validate, and improve solutions rapidly. *The Lean Startup* by Eric Ries and associated work by Ries and Steve Blank are now required reading for any budding entrepreneur. And rightfully so: its lessons are simple and powerful. However, the concept of fast learning iterations, early validation, and minimal prototypes that illustrate key but bare-bones functionality are not new. The Wright brothers, the Apple I computer from 1976, and Microsoft's early efforts with both MITS and Apple are all examples of a lean start-up methodology. Within large firms, these philosophies are starting to take hold, too. Information technology firms like Constant Contact and Citrix are exploring how internally funded start-up teams can create new businesses. So far, the results have been promising.[19] For the venture mode, establishing an entrepreneurial culture, building the infrastructure, and giving teams the resources and support they need to develop concepts are essential, but these aspects also remain a challenge. Unfortunately, many of the firms we researched experiment in the venture mode, have success, but have their efforts fizzle out and not become engrained in the organization or culture. The EMC example is different, as they committed to the process long term, enhanced it, and made it a sustainable initiative across the organization.

In chapter 8, in the network mode, internal teams rely heavily on outsiders for innovation, so it's all about coordination. Here, in the venture mode, the two forces allow the teams to do many of the activities themselves. Easy-to-use CAD allows even those non-engineers to express their designs in fully functioning models. Software tools allow laymen to create very realistic mock-ups of apps and websites. As we discussed under resource control, some teams may want to learn new skills. For example, someone in technical sales may learn how to put together a credible app mock-up. Others might learn CAD and how to use a 3D printer. In other cases, hiring a freelance industrial designer may make more sense for project speed. As we discussed earlier, having a hyper-functional team with overall control and decision-making responsibility is essential. They can make the determination about who does what and when.

Level 3: Implementation

Incentives

Inside large companies, the incentives have to be designed such that they fit into the overall culture. The best innovation teams are those that are empowered to go inside and outside corporate walls to succeed. The hyper-functional teams, which can leverage the best of what new ventures do well, do what's needed to "move the ball down the field." It is essential that management give teams the support and freedom to operate in this fashion. Without it, they are just skunkworks teams constrained inside the same corporate bounds.[20] Autonomy and empowerment are powerful incentives. This is a foundational incentive for this mode.

What about the money? While cash prizes are part of the equation, equally powerful – if not more so – are reputational signals. For example, EMC (before the merger with Dell) was similar to many technical companies in that they already had a system of fellows and distinguished engineers – titles and positions that conveyed high status. EMC assigned some of them to support selected internal venture teams. This way the visibility of the distinguished personnel lent credibility to the people working on the ideas. Similarly, widely publicized career advances of people who worked in these internal start-up teams send powerful signals to the entire organization. Winners of their Innovation Network project idea contests are given company-wide recognition, then given time to develop these entrepreneurial projects. No extra bonuses or stock options. Just time, and the satisfaction of leading your own efforts. Simple and effective.

New KPIs

Here's where some interesting things can be done. Because one of the main benefits of the venture mode is an increase in the number of innovation opportunities and concepts being developed, a series of KPIs can be developed around this. First, tracking the number of ventures is important, as are employee participation rates and of course how the projects progress. This includes development speed, as well as tracking the success percentages as they travel through the process of concept development, customer validation, and amount of internal investment raised. Last, the percentage of new revenue generated by these new projects is essential.

Within the venture development process, there are other KPIs that are more subtle but still vital. Lean start-up methods prescribe the development of functional prototypes to test and validate ideas early, refine, and pivot as needed. Developing a minimally functional prototype (MVP) is a good philosophy, but new technology allows quick and inexpensive development of very credible prototypes. These need to be tested and validated and need to be part of the KPI suite. Examples include painted 3D-printed prototypes that look and feel like a final product or clean and slick software demos. If you are interfacing with lead users, investors, or lead channel partners, spending just a little more time leveraging new prototyping technology to have a more resolved MVP can make the difference. As part of the venture mentoring network, having coaches from design and marketing can add a critical eye as concept designs are pushed forward. However, be careful to manage design iterations, as digital technology can foster a culture of endless iterations and churn.[21]

Summary

The perfect storm of digital tools and a collaborative culture has expanded the opportunity for individual entrepreneurs and small teams to rapidly develop, test, and validate product and service concepts extremely cost-effectively through the use of new tools and services. Firms can unlock the same potential of their own employees by establishing an infrastructure that supports and a culture that encourages internal venturing. This system allows the development of empowered hyper-functional teams, which can operate inside and outside the corporation to assemble and control the resources needed to develop their vision. These teams need autonomy, flexibility, and decision-making authority. They need support, education, and mentoring. Upper-level and C-suite executives also play a critical role, ensuring long-term support for space, funding, and the incentives to keep employees engaged as they, from the ground up, develop potential transformative business ideas. We have seen many examples, the most notable being EMC, where this system worked effectively. And the venture mode augments existing new product and service development funnels, increasing the number of opportunities and concepts being worked on within the corporation. It's simply a very cost-effective way to spur innovation and increase employee engagement.

Key Points

- The venture mode expands the innovation landscape to individual and small teams through a collection of new digital tools and services.
- Established firms can learn from start-ups and implement a new venture system to encourage and support these projects.
- The ventures increase the number of seeds in your innovation process and can engage employees outside of traditional R&D.
- The venture infrastructure needs to give hyper-functional teams empowerment, financial support, and direct control over their destiny.

- A venturing process that includes milestones, seed funding, education, and mentoring is essential, as is eschewing corporate bureaucracy.
- Recognition and satisfaction are important incentives.

Assessments

As with the previous chapters, let's see where you are and where your skills need to be advanced. Please answer the following questions on your current activities within the venture mode with a focus on entrepreneurial infrastructure, processes, and culture:

- Does your organization encourage employees to develop their own innovation opportunities, even if they are not in R&D?
- Do you have a way for small teams to form and develop new ideas?
- If so, are they allowed to be autonomous and have direct control of decisions and resources?
- Do you provide investment to new ventures outside of R&D?
- Are employees allowed a percentage of time to develop new ideas?
- Do you have a defined method for providing resources (education, mentoring, etc.) to venture teams?
- Do you have space for venture teams?
- Are there incentives provided to employees to contribute new ideas to the organization?
- Do you measure the quantity and quality of new ideas being developed both in existing R&D programs and generally within the corporation?

For More Information

For further reading, please see the following:

Marion, Tucker, Denise D. Dunlap, and John H. Friar. "Instilling the Entrepreneurial Spirit in Your R&D Team: What Large Firms Can Learn from Successful Start-ups." *IEEE Transactions on Engineering Management* 59, no. 2 (2012): 323–37.

Marion, Tucker J. "Innovation Management: Making Lean Innovation Work." *CIMS Management Report*, January/February 2017. https://cims.ncsu.edu /cims_newsletter/januaryfebruary-2/innovation-management-making -lean-innovation-work/.

Smith, Calvin, Sebastian K. Fixson, Carlos Paniagua-Ferrari, and Salvatore Parise. "The Evolution of an Innovation Capability: Making Internal Idea Competitions Work in a Large Enterprise: One Firm Evolved Its Idea Competitions into a Broad Innovation Management System." *Research-Technology Management* 60, no. 2 (2017): 26–35.

The Community Mode

In contrast to the specialist and venture innovation modes, which both focused on activities and structures internal to the firm, the community innovation mode bridges firm boundaries by also engaging outsiders in the innovation process. It does so, however, without the firm having the type of control that typical contracting in supply chains usually carries. Rather than using direct authority, in the community mode firms employ a wide range of incentive mechanisms to coordinate work among the various partners, notably crossing firm boundaries.

As with the other modes in the expanded innovation landscape, the emergence of our two major forces – digital design and social collaboration – are prime enablers for this mode. In fact, although the mechanics for a subset of approaches in the community mode are centuries old, recent advancements in digital design technologies have dramatically multiplied its occurrences. More specifically, modern digital design technologies support the community mode of innovation in two ways. First, as we discussed in chapter 2, the steadily decreasing cost of owning, using, and learning digital design software and fabrication technology has lowered the barrier to entry so far that today many more people can and do engage in design activities than could do so even a decade ago. Second, the falling communication costs for transferring messages and data files between collaborating parties have made collaboration comparatively easy. In addition, the emergence of social media has only accelerated these trends. As a result, communities have sprung up that include a whole range of expertise, from those fairly new to the technology to seasoned veterans. And many of these communities have strong egalitarian and meritocratic notions. Consider, for example, the community of engineering designers GrabCAD. Founded in 2009 by Estonians Hardi Meybaum and Indrek Narusk as a marketplace to connect engineers with CAD-related jobs, it quickly grew into a platform for engineers to share CAD models. Now headquartered in Cambridge, Massachusetts, in 2013, GrabCAD added WorkBench, a cloud-based collaboration solution, and turned into a collaboration platform for CAD designers.[1] GrabCAD also ran numerous design competitions for its community. Its egalitarian structure attracted many young designers and engineering students. In September 2014, 3D-printing giant Stratasys bought GrabCAD, reportedly for a sum of $100 million.[2]

Some variants of the community mode of innovation have recently emerged under the heading of open innovation, a term coined by Henry Chesbrough in his 2003 book of the same name.[3] The major premise underlying open innovation is the insight that "no matter who you are, the smartest people probably work for someone else."[4] This insight raises the question of how to find these people. As it turns out, auction-style setups, so-called innovation contests, are a very efficient way to do this as long as they attract the right people to self-select into the pool of participants.

The insight itself that underlies innovation contests is not really new. Records show that this mechanism had already been employed more than 300 years ago. For example, in the early 1700s the British Navy was losing too many ships due to navigation errors. The main problem was that there was no reliable way to identify the longitude of a ship's position, and no one within the British Navy could solve this problem. As a result, in 1714 the British government set out a price of £20,000 for a solution that would enable measuring the longitude of a ship's position at sea to a pre-specified degree of accuracy. In those days, communication was slow and expensive, so it took time for a solution to be developed, tested, and accepted as the winner. In 1761, clockmaker John Harrison claimed the prize.

In the time since, open calls for innovation contests have been used successfully on numerous occasions. From prizes for flying across the Atlantic Ocean in the 1920s, to their modern equivalents, the XPRIZE, innovation contests have a track record of attracting the talent and abilities of the outside population, be they individuals or firms.[5] What makes today's situation unique is that the two forces make it possible for firms to co-create with a large outside community of individuals on a never-seen-before scale.

As a manager responsible for innovation, one can access these communities today via intermediaries as needed. For example, when ExxonMobil during the cleanup of an oil spill ran into a problem – they could not pump oil from barges that sat in frigid water – they posted this problem on the site of innovation intermediary InnoCentive. InnoCentive in turn posted the challenge to its global community including hundreds of thousands of scientists and engineers (over 375,000 as of November 2016).[6] A civil engineer who saw the problem noticed its similarity to preventing concrete from solidifying before it is deployed at the construction site. The answer for that problem: vibration (which is why you see concrete delivery trucks equipped with mechanisms to rotate their giant drums). After the engineer proposed this solution, some oil engineers built a giant "stir" to test the idea and confirmed that the engineer's solution solved their problem.

This mechanism, the assumption that someone else already has the solution to your problem, is at the heart of innovation contests of the kind that InnoCentive organizes. In fact, the results of a survey among over 1,100 solution providers published by NineSigma, one of InnoCentive's competitors as an innovation intermediary,[7] confirm this effect: most solution providers state that either the problem for which they submitted a solution fell "inside my core field of expertise" or their submission was "based on an existing solution." As a result, almost two-thirds of solution providers estimate the time it took them to develop their solution as "less than one week."[8]

On the other side of the spectrum is the potential to engage with users and customers who may not be experts but rather enthusiasts and people with simple interest and curiosity. This can be via social media platforms such as Facebook and LinkedIn, or a custom platform such as the one developed by Quirky. The promise of open innovation is just that – easy access and engagement with many people. An example is Unilever. Unilever has an open innovation portal where it asks the general population to solve pertinent issues like intelligent packaging.[9] Interestingly, some recent research has shown that social media and its impact on innovation have not lived up to expectations.[10] A detailed investigation into Quirky noted that while the community developed many incremental ideas, none were earth-shattering in terms of customer reviews and most were not leaders in their market segment.

However, given the success of idea hunts and solution services, and the enthusiastic communities developed at firms ranging from GrabCAD to IBM,[11] open innovation has tremendous value. But what is important is the strategy you and your firm need to take as you develop this mode, experiment, and integrate the community into your innovation process. In this chapter we'll discuss the unique attributes of this mode, and how the Six Factors should be considered in its development and exploitation.

Level 1: Mode Foundations

Resource Control
Not surprisingly, the level of resource control in the innovation community mode is lower from the perspective of the focal firm. In fact, the mechanism that makes the community innovation mode work is far better described with terms like "curation" or "orchestration" than with "control." That said, digital design tools can play an important role in managing this process. Consider, for example, the previously mentioned Local Motors, a company operating firmly in the community mode and using its community to inform both the problem and the solution space. Local Motors, founded in 2007 in Phoenix, Arizona, is a transportation company focused on community-based design and local, small-scale manufacturing. It developed a digital system, called the Forge, which links outside contributors (enthusiasts, engineers, designers, and makers) with internal firm design challenges. By 2013, their community of contributors reached 30,000, with another 50,000 available to have input on designs via social media.[12] Their first vehicle, the Rally Fighter off-road vehicle, used many parts designed by the community and was ultimately fabricated by Local Motors in one of their small factories. The Forge eventually developed into a co-creation platform that today is project-centric and has specific categories where the community can contribute and co-create. These include challenges for technical solutions, which reside in the solution space of the innovation process (Figure 6.1), and requests for new project ideas (called "Sparks"), discussions, and brainstorms, which reside in the

problem space of the innovation process. This community platform is not only arranged to assist Local Motors' internal projects but is also a tool where outside firms contract with Local Motors to develop ideas and vehicle solutions. Local Motors has developed projects for Peterbilt trucks, BMW, Airbus, Domino's Pizza, and others. It is clear that Local Motors has invested a great deal of effort in designing and managing its digital platform to best leverage and manage its community. It handles postings, collaboration between users, ratings and feedback, and project management activities. For managers looking to replicate this model, this will require substantial time, support, and resources.

In the problem space, many firms try to leverage existing social media platforms like Facebook as a quick and easy way to try open innovation and community interaction. And the draw is there. It's relatively easy to set up a company Facebook page, amass a group of customers, and seek input on new product ideas. A word of caution, however: just because you are on social media does not mean you will successfully leverage the community to benefit your innovation efforts. Different approaches are needed for each social media platform, and research suggests that the strategy taken, a social strategy, is key to developing, engaging, and cultivating a community that is a source of knowledge for innovation.[13]

Intellectual Property

In most cases the owner of the innovation competition sets clear rules up-front and dictates those rules. For example, in the case of Quirky, the rules for submitting an idea were clear: if the idea were selected and fully developed into a commercial product, the firm owned the idea and the community and inventor would receive compensation. Other firms take a different approach. Local Motors' former CIO noted in 2013, "We're the opposite (of a traditional company). We have a creative comments clause. If they post it, they own it. If you want to move really quickly, that's the most important. Rather than going out and getting patents. We're not trying to protect everything. As a matter of fact, everything we did in designing the Rally Fighter, we published on the Website."[14] For managers of traditional firms, most of which are specialists, this is antithetical to the core principles of technology ownership and the profits earned therein. However, from the Android developer community to SAP to SpaceX's Hyperloop project, many firms leverage open source for product lines or entire divisions. So when deliberating whether and how to use the community mode, IP needs to be a consideration. But also to be considered is a different, more open approach to ownership that promotes sharing and collaboration among the community. This approach essentially strives to enlarge the pie, rather than changing the allocation of who gets what. Regardless of approach and strategy for IP, the mechanisms and guidelines for interfacing with the community need to be clearly defined. For example, at Airbus Helicopters, their open innovation portal has an extensive list of general conditions that outline any engagement and disclosure of information.[15]

Level 2: Organizational Development

Organizational Design
The level of involvement and desired engagement in this mode and its impact on how community efforts affect the organization cannot be underestimated. Running simple contests or posting idea hunts on Facebook is certainly low cost and easy to implement, as we discussed. However, in many ways you get what you pay for. Simply trying to access social media is not a means to improve your innovation efforts. We discussed a defined social strategy, one that cultivates and motivates the community. Engagement with a community can

be viewed as a continuum. On one side, you have simple idea contests hosted on your website and perhaps accessed via social media. On the other end is a well-defined and integrated platform that develops a community along the lines of Local Motors or Quirky. But this is expensive and difficult to do, as noted in chapter 1. Quirky ran through over $150 million in venture capital funds to develop and sustain its community-based ecosystem. As we mentioned previously, this requires investment, staffing, management, and a defined system of performance metrics.

For the innovation manager, the community mode offers great potential, but don't forget the integration challenge! How the firm interacts with the community, the level of access, and the intensity of collaboration are important considerations. We have seen with Quirky the difficulty managing a community and the various stakeholders in the problem space and solution space. Quirky's process was unique in that its model combined elements of both competition and collaboration. In an ongoing process, every member could submit ideas ("problems" in our framework). From this idea pool, a small number were selected through a two-phase process. First, when ideas were posted, the community commented on them, sometimes combined them, and ultimately rated them on a point system. Those ideas that floated to the top then entered the second step: an evaluation at which a combination of management and community made the final selection decision. After the company had selected a problem to work on, it broke down the actual product development work into a number of mini-contests on concept designs, naming possibilities, and design issues. The community was invited to participate in these mini-contests, incentivized by the opportunity to earn influence points, which could later translate into cash payments (this work is positioned in the "solution space" in our innovation process model, highlighted by the small orange boxes in Figure 6.1). At this point, when these contests such as color schemes and names were established, Quirky then relied on internal designers and engineers to finish the product design for mass production.

As companies experiment with the community mode more frequently, the analysis of open innovation outcomes at established organizations often finds that external ideas die within the existing structures of the firm; that is, they do not receive the support required to develop them into market-ready products.[16] The logic of the open innovation portion of the process seems to be too different from the command-and-control process that exists in most companies to execute ideas.[17] On some level, the existing organization tries to protect its internal order against ideas entering from outside the company and kills ideas that often challenge established power and resource structures. Our detailed analysis of Quirky's innovation process – with its heavy emphasis on open innovation since its inception – seems to indicate the same problem, just viewed from the opposite end. A company's back end of a process that designs and manufactures goods must be able to control the volume and diversity of incoming ideas to ensure that the existing capacity can actually produce quality output in a timely manner. In the case of Quirky, instead of the back-end process limiting incoming ideas from the outside, it appears that the back-end process became overwhelmed by the demand the open innovation front end placed on it. Compounding the problem were financial commitments to the community in both the problem and solution spaces.

As managers implement a community mode, the balance of community and internal involvement in both the problem and solution spaces are all-important. Quirky relied on the community for the problem space in somewhat of a hands-off fashion, then fed the community some nuggets of influence of the design, while the internal team did the hard part of developing a manufacturing-ready product. And, as we mentioned, the internal team was overwhelmed by the volume of incoming ideas from the upstream community. As juxtaposition, Local Motors is more of a co-creation effort, where internal and external resources share in design, which is very carefully parsed and executed. Process discipline needs to be a focus, and if the community is engaged, the parameters and outcomes need to have specificity. Finally, the overall organizational design, knowledge, and project management system needs to be robust. Digital-design software providers are answering this call. At PTC, the company's next-generation ThingWorx technology platform is designed to foster communities of developers to collect, analyze, and leverage large amounts of data from connected products and systems. According to PTC, the company's solutions are deployed in more than 26,000 businesses worldwide to generate a product or service advantage.[18]

Task Allocation

A defining characteristic of the community innovation mode is that, of course, the locus of innovation is somewhere out in the community, and seldom inside the company. That being said, there are different communities that can hold the locus of innovation, depending on the nature of what the community can deliver. Recall the general innovation process that conceptualizes the innovation process as consisting of two parts: one part exploring the problem space, the other part exploring the solution space (as shown in Figure 6.1). InnoCentive, NineSigma, or yet2 all live in the solution space, in which the innovation contests support the parallel generation of concepts and potential answers to carefully worded problem statements, or challenges (the right side of Figure 6.1). These innovation contests can work well for innovation problems that start from a well-defined problem and for which a technical solution can be found, evaluated, and selected.

So if you as an innovation manager can craft a focused problem statement, for which you would like those entities that may hold a

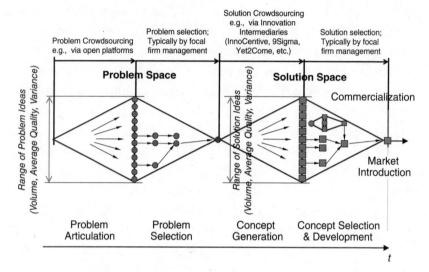

Figure 6.1: Innovation process model.
© 2018 Tucker J. Marion, Sebastian K. Fixson

solution to your problem to self-select as providers, then you should consider an innovation contest. This is the area of the innovation process where innovation intermediaries such as InnoCentive and NineSigma predominantly play.

But innovation contests also exist in the problem space (the left side of Figure 6.1), although they are less straightforward because it is more difficult for users to articulate a problem than it is for technical experts to describe a solution. One way around this challenge is to allow users to describe their need through their own solution ideas. For example, in the spring of 2015, Procter & Gamble asked its customers to "envision the ideal shopping experience." On its surface, this question asks for solutions, but really it tried to get at the underlying challenges that might motivate a customer to propose a certain solution.

As an illustration, look at the three winning submissions of this contest: an online recommendation system that can be trusted, a vending machine that sells both large and small portions of the same product, and a shopping cart whose features accelerate the process of finding and paying for purchases. It may be that some of the technical features of these suggestions were relevant and interesting, but far more important are the needs and problems for which these solutions merely served as a vehicle to be expressed: the problem of needing trusted advice when choosing products, the varying consumption patterns at (or near) a single location (either via different people or via the same people at different times), and the still-taxing efforts as shoppers to do the work of identifying and purchasing goods in a supermarket setting.[19]

So for managers, understanding where different open innovation and community involvement can play a role is essential. The previous examples show that targeted use of open innovation can be very effective in each space. The challenge for this mode is to have the same community play a role in both the problem space and the solution space simultaneously. This is where Quirky lived and where a firm like Local Motors is exploring.

When thinking about task allocation, who does what within and outside the firm is a critical area to plan when developing the community mode. Are you asking the community for limited feedback on ideas and concepts? Or do you want to deeply engage and co-develop solutions with them? The fundamental strategy of task allocation is directly related to the overall mission of the community mode endeavor. In this chapter, we mentioned a continuum of community engagement and development, beginning with social media and progressing to a sophisticated custom platform that is the hub of community activity (like GrabCAD or Local Motor's website).

There are varying levels of sophistication in firms' approaches to social media (SM) and the development of the community mode.

Even if you decide to use an outside firm like InnoCentive for an issue with a solution, we recommend that you begin the path of internal skill development in your firm. The development of the community mode should follow a capability maturity model, in which the development of capabilities can be more formalized and mature over time. We propose a multilevel framework in terms of sophistication and capability that can be applied to the development of an engaged community. An easy place to start is with your SM efforts. At Level 1, firms have little or no social media presence. At Level 2, some SM presence is seen, with firms having Facebook pages and Twitter accounts. At Level 3, firms may actively post and tweet, but beyond product promotion, nothing is done to promote a well-conceived social strategy and engagement with the community for innovation. At Level 4, firms have developed well-defined and well-deployed SM and community engagement capabilities, where they are not only actively adding content and promotion but also posting content of general interest to the community, integrating idea hunts and contents into the fold, and proactively integrating customers into the innovation process for co-creation. At Level 5, the business model is actually centered on fully developed SM and community mode capabilities combined with an extremely engaged and incentivized community. This level may require custom, private platforms or enhanced mobile applications (e.g., the Starbucks App or Local Motors' platform) to interact with users. In addition, the community may be given financial incentives to foster contribution (this is discussed in more detail in the next section). Local Motors and Autodesk are examples of this level from the vantage of custom community platforms. Levels 4 and 5 are areas where outside communities are tasked with greater responsibility of design and input into the project. A graphic of the community mode capabilities framework is shown in Figure 6.2.

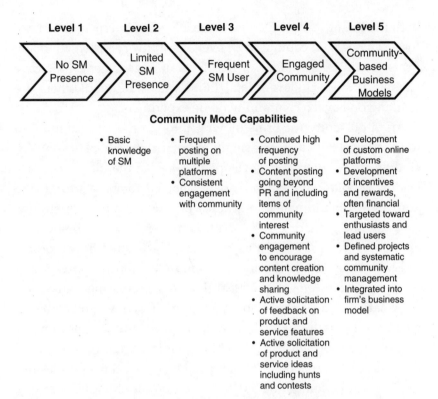

Community Mode Capabilities

Level 1	Level 2	Level 3	Level 4	Level 5
	• Basic knowledge of SM	• Frequent posting on multiple platforms • Consistent engagement with community	• Continued high frequency of posting • Content posting going beyond PR and including items of community interest • Community engagement to encourage content creation and knowledge sharing • Active solicitation of feedback on product and service features • Active solicitation of product and service ideas including hunts and contests	• Development of custom online platforms • Development of incentives and rewards, often financial • Targeted toward enthusiasts and lead users • Defined projects and systematic community management • Integrated into firm's business model

Figure 6.2: Community mode capabilities framework.

From Tucker J. Marion, Deborah Roberts, Gloria Barczak, and Marina Candi, "Developing Social Strategies for NPD: A Capability Model Framework" (conference proceeding, International Product Development Management Conference, Copenhagen, Denmark, June 14–16, 2015). Note that an early version of the capabilities framework was presented in proceedings at the 2015 IPDM conference.

Developing fully realized community mode capabilities takes effort, and generating high levels of interaction and original content consumes resources (either internal or external, with creating the posts, finding articles to link, etc.). Firms need to be committed with both marketing and R&D to generate a level of interaction that can foster an engaged community. Level 5 is still very rare, with many firms "testing the waters" of that level of engagement. Procter & Gamble (P&G), Unilever, Tata, Lindt Chocolate, and others are working on Level 5 community mode experiments.[20]

An opportunity for firms moving through the skill continuum toward Level 5 is the increasingly important mobile platforms, including those internally developed. For example, Starbucks is a leading mobile payment provider. Their customer platform (the app) allows an intimate interaction with users and the community, all the while gathering streams of data useful to new innovation efforts. A former CTO of a leading travel site noted in one of our interviews that "the real value of communities and your business is that they become *intertwined*. Real-time data processing, behavioral information and patterns, and custom pathways when combined with mobile platforms make the event powerful and meaningful for both the user and firm."[21] While open-innovation-centric business models like that of Local Motors may not be realistic or desired for most firms, combining SM and a community-building strategy to enhance the overall business model is something all firms should consider. Today there are various providers of open innovation solutions, which range from executing innovation contests with large consumer communities to running ideation sessions with internal employees to managing supplier innovation events. Examples include companies like Imaginatik (www.imaginatik.com) in Boston and Hyve (www.hyve.net) in Munich.

Level 3: Implementation

Incentives

Given the firm boundary-crossing nature and the absence of direct control mechanisms in the community innovation mode, the question of why people participate in it in the first place deserves special consideration. Motivational theory says that incentives can occur across a broad spectrum: from purely extrinsic, typically exemplified by monetary compensation (e.g., prize money in an auction-style setting such as InnoCentive), to purely intrinsic (for example, many contribute for the improvement of openly available resources, such as the open source community).

While it appears as if these motivational extremes are endpoints of a dichotomy – with extrinsic motivations such as money, status, and fame on one end and intrinsic motivations such as altruistic behavior, learning, or enjoyment on the other – closer inspection tells us that though there is some trade-off occurring at the frontier, many recent business models do in fact employ a mix of extrinsic and intrinsic incentives (see Figure 6.3).

On one end of the spectrum are intermediaries for innovation – i.e., such firms as InnoCentive, NineSigma, and yet2. In those models, the cash incentive is the major motivator, and the relationships tend to be more transactional. In fact, in many cases, the solution seeker and the solution provider never meet; they remain anonymous to each other, with their transactions being facilitated by the intermediary.

On the other end of the spectrum are innovation community models such as open source communities. In these settings there is no economic prize to be won; rather, working on a project larger than oneself motivates most participants. For repeated participation, often belonging to the community itself becomes the central motivator.

Between these extremes fall business models that combine extrinsic and intrinsic motivation. For example, companies such as Threadless provide prize money as an economic incentive, but in many cases the expected value of winning these prizes is so small that a rational economic actor would not participate. Instead, the firms provide their communities of participants with avenues and mechanisms

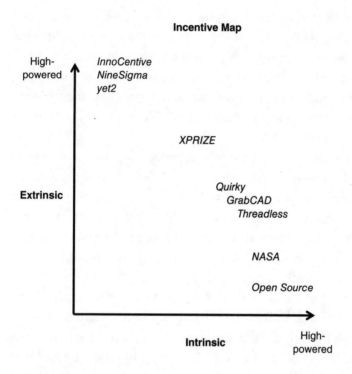

Figure 6.3: Combination of extrinsic and intrinsic motivations.
© 2018 Tucker J. Marion, Sebastian K. Fixson

for rich online social interactions, both among participants and between participants and the firm. To accomplish this requires a social strategy as mentioned in the last section. This is why developing mode capabilities to motivate and engage the community is so essential. In some cases, this approach has led to communities more than one million members strong.

This mix of extrinsic and intrinsic incentives requires managing a careful balance between collaboration as a community and competing as a company. Consider the words of former Local Motors chief information officer Tim Thomas: "There is crowd sourcing and co-creation. In terms of co-creation we think of it as a process where we're working with the community. We're sort of mixed in with them. As opposed to crowd sourcing, where we're going to pick stuff out of the community and take it from you. In our model, we definitely give back and work together."[22]

A recent example from Local Motors illustrates the mix of motivators within the process: the Urban Mobility Challenge: Berlin 2030. The winning design came from a 24-year-old designer from Colombia. The designer received $20,000 for his efforts. The project, now named Olli, is a self-driving vehicle for urban transportation; it is being developed with the community. Multiple challenges have been posted, ranging from the design of the exterior door to vehicle suspension systems (these projects are not compensated but rated by the community). As the Olli project and others continue development, the status of challenges is updated, as are ideas and design solutions from the community. This is done via their website, and the updates are shared much like a wiki such as Basecamp. Interestingly, while Local Motors states, "We invite any and all people to solve the world's most challenging problems," from our research we found that the community has a high degree of skills in design and engineering. This is somewhat different from the case of Quirky discussed in chapter 2, which had a similar mission but appeared to have created a community with significant lower levels of technical expertise in new product development.

New KPIs
Once you have implemented a community-centric innovation model, how do you measure its value and success? Since this is an innovation process question, the overall metrics are the same. How long did the effort take and how much did it cost? For the former, we know that many people involved can make quick work of a

problem. In comparing Quirky's process to a standard, internally developed product, we found their up-front problem space and ultimate concept selection process was more efficient than a small, dedicated internal team. However, overall development was not faster, as the result of resource constraints and managing the involvement of the community in all the small design challenges (managing and integrating all the small orange boxes in Figures 1.1 or 6.1). A graphic of the innovation timeline comparing one of Quirky's products to a competitor is shown in Figure 6.4.

We suggest that for community-based projects, timing needs to be segmented by process step, with the understanding that overall cycle time may not improve. Some items may be fast, but ultimately co-creation and integration with the community may take longer than with a dedicated internal team. Related to speed is cost. However, one of the benefits of the community mode is the potential for many resources to be involved at low cost. Even with incentives to the community, overall cost may be lower. Think of all the designers on GrabCAD, who purchase and maintain their own laptops, design software, and internet connections. This is effectively a large reduction in fixed costs for the firm leveraging these communities.

A good metric to consider are the total number (quantity), quality, and diversity of problems and solutions developed in the community mode. For example, one of the benefits of the community in both the problem and the solution space is the volume of contributions. As we have seen in idea hunts and efforts such as Quirky's, there is no shortage of knowledge created by the community. This is important to measure. But perhaps more important is the quality of the knowledge created. While difficult to measure, this quality can be assessed by the community as well as the internal team members who curate and manage the process. Well-managed community mode examples usually have a combination of both. Finally, the diversity of ideas is important. Increasing diversity can be directly

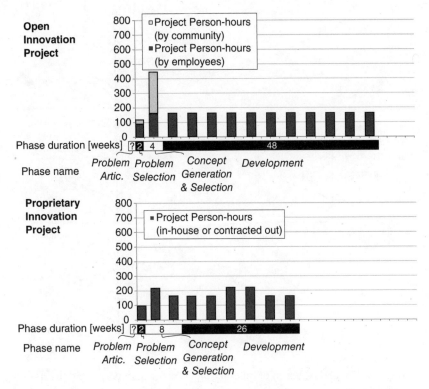

Figure 6.4: Development person hours, open innovation versus closed.

related to the breadth and expertise of the community. To visualize these metrics and the interaction of these three important characteristics, one can view the results of the community output as shown in the schematic in Figure 6.5.

In implementing the community mode, managers should pay attention to formulating and formalizing these metrics, and should establish dashboards as shown in Figure 6.5 to track and evaluate the knowledge created. This may ultimately help the firm decide where and when the community and open innovation efforts have the greatest impact on the innovation process.

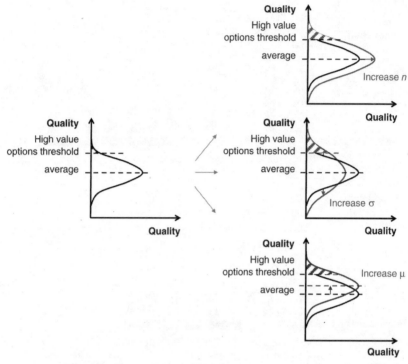

Figure 6.5: Visual dashboard of quantity (n), average quality (μ), and diversity (σ) of an idea pool.

Adapted from Fixson and Marion, "When Innovation Stumbles"; Sebastian K. Fixson and Tucker J. Marion, "How Much Better Is Open Innovation?" (symposium presentation at the Academy of Management, Los Angeles, CA, August 5–9, 2016).

Summary

The combination of digital design and ease with which people can communicate and collaborate has allowed the formation of communities of unprecedented scale and speed. These communities make the promise of more open innovation a reality. While firms like GE and P&G are experimenting with this mode, it is still in its infancy. Companies like Local Motors, Quirky, InnoCentive, and others have carved out unique positions in either the problem space or the solution space, and sometimes in both. What this means for managers is that this is fertile ground to explore, but it is not as simple as tapping into a Facebook group for ideas. It will take skill development, a commitment to develop the community, a robust platform to collaborate with and manage the community, and an understanding of where and when open innovation and the community should be applied to both idea generation and solution development. It is here, in the intelligent application of open innovation, where firms can gain the most from the community mode.

Key Points

- The community mode has enormous potential to impact certain aspects of the innovation process. It can be the source of many low-cost problems or solutions.
- However, the quality of solutions from the general population can be limited.
- Communities of experts can be useful to work on issues of higher difficulty and can be helpful during the solution space.
- Incentives can raise the level of quality, but too much incentive can be detrimental as it impacts the participant pool negatively. Some firms are seeing that recognition and rewards are beneficial.
- Relying on the community mode for the entire process might not be wise. But at certain points, integration can be very useful.

Assessments

Let's see where you are and where your skills need to be advanced. Please answer the following questions on your current activities within the community mode, rating these on a scale of 1–5 (1 being "not at all" and 5 being "extensively").

- Does your company have a presence on social media (e.g., Facebook, Twitter, etc.)?
- Do you engage with users and customers on social media?
- Do you ask for new product or service ideas or for feedback on social media?
- Are your approaches to social media and the community systematic and well-integrated with your marketing and innovation departments?
- Do you offer contests and prizes to your community?
- Do you engage with any outside open innovation firms (like InnoCentive)?

Please answer these questions about developing your community mode, rating your answers on a scale of 1–5 (1 being "not at all" and 5 being "extensively").

- How much do you need to focus on improving your problem space (e.g., generating new ideas)?
- Do you need to improve your solution space (getting to designs and solutions faster)?
- Do you need to improve both the problem and the solution space concurrently?
- Do you have a substantial budget to develop a custom online platform for building and managing a community?

- Is IP important to your firm/division/SBU?
- Are you willing to bring outsiders into key decisions for product and part features?
- How valuable is idea volume to your innovation efforts?
- How valuable are the quality of the ideas?
- How much are you willing to pay the outside community for their contributions?

As with previous chapters, if you have a low score on this assessment, let's say below 10, you need work. Have your team concentrate on mode development by considering the key points and assessment items outlined above.

For More Information

For further reading and exercises, please see the following.

Chesbrough, Henry W. *Open Innovation: The New Imperative for Creating and Profiting from Technology*. Cambridge, MA: Harvard Business Press, 2006.
Fixson, Sebastian K., and Tucker J. Marion. "A Case Study of Crowdsourcing Gone Wrong." *Harvard Business Review*, December 15, 2016, https://hbr.org/2016/12/a-case-study-of-crowdsourcing-gone-wrong.
Marion, Tucker J., Deborah Roberts, Marina Candi, and Gloria Barczak. "Customizing Your Social Strategy to the Platform." *MIT Sloan Management Review*, March 30, 2016.

The Network Mode

In previous chapters we have discussed the performance benefits specialists can realize by fully embracing the two forces, how firms can become more entrepreneurial by enabling a system of internal venturing, and the potential of the community to affect the innovation process. In this chapter, we discuss the network mode – a mode that combines sharing and selective collaborative interactions with high-performance product design. This mode goes well beyond outsourcing and contractual supplier relationships and is the development of a new, coordinated ecosystem of partners ranging from universities to start-ups, working in concert to realize an innovation. This mode increases the richness of innovation solutions and, if managed properly, can increase speed and lower costs. In a 2017 article in *Fortune*, the Allergan CEO discussed the importance of an innovation network and outside collaboration. He states, "If we walk outside, we're fishing in an ocean vs. a pond for innovation."[1] The network mode – for specialists – in many ways is the most logical next step in exploring the expanded innovation landscape.

But first, a little history. Globalization, offshoring, and outsourcing are a hot-button issue as this book is being written. The current political climate has put an emphasis on trade agreements, and the perceived negative impact from a labor perspective on First World countries such as the United Kingdom and the United States. Let's first look at offshoring. With the passing of NAFTA in the 1990s and the admission of China to the World Trade Organization in 2001, organizations looking to reduce costs accelerated the move to manufacturing offshore. From toys to consumer electronics to car parts, firms realized the benefits of labor costs that overseas could be many times less than fully allocated hourly costs in developed economies such as the United States or Germany.[2] For example, in 2002, US average hourly compensation was $21.11, almost 33 times higher than in China.[3] If you were in the business of making products that required hand assembly, there really was no way a US-based operation could compete. This even affected design itself; with low assembly costs, design for automation and assembly became less of a concern.[4] Production tooling, with steel subsidized by the Chinese government, could be up to 50 percent less expensive than in the United States. For executives, offshoring was really a "no brainer" from an operational cost perspective. Go into a big-box store such as Target, and with the exception of food, drugs, and large items, nearly all the products are produced or assembled in Asia.[5] In late 2016, the first Chinese-made vehicle began to be sold in the United States – the GM Buick Envision.[6] Unless there is a dramatic shift in trade and tax policies, many more will follow. In 2011, Apple CEO Steve Jobs famously told President Obama, "the jobs aren't coming back."[7] From a company perspective, the last 20 years of accelerated globalization and sourcing location have been a big positive to the bottom line.

The second factor in considering the historical development of the network mode is outsourcing. Up until the 1980s, most specialists were vertically integrated. From internal component sourcing to manufacturing and assembly, the original equipment manufacturer (OEM) typically produced many if not most of the components and subsystems that constituted the final product. Just look at Apple. In 1984, Apple launched the Macintosh (Mac) computer to great fanfare. Along with the launch was a new Apple factory in Fremont, California.[8] Highly automated, this factory could produce a new Mac every 27 seconds. The Mac production line was eventually moved to another facility in California, but the plant remained open until 1992 making computer printers. With Steve Jobs back at Apple in 1998 and current CEO Tim Cook leading supply chain transformation, Apple began to shed its manufacturing operations, instead focusing on its core competencies of design and hardware/software integration. The first product to fully realize this new, core focus was the iPod. While it is of course no longer a core Apple product, the history of iPod's development is essential to understanding the importance of the network mode.

In developing the iPod (and the iPhone that followed), Apple took many cues from the venture mode but realized the product through its nascent network mode. The iPod project was led by a small development team. The project manager, Tony Fadell (of recent Nest fame), was an outside contractor. Fadell worked with internal personnel such as Jonathan Ive (design), Stan Ng (marketing), and Jon Rubinstein (hardware and software) to develop the concept and product. The initial iPod prototype was developed in six weeks.[9] The team worked extensively with their external suppliers and internal technology departments to arrange the necessary technology and components. This included small hard drives from Toshiba and microcontrollers from ARM. In-house industrial design was performed, as was development of the software. But their network *ecosystem* also included key technologies from new, smaller ventures, such as critical MP3 software from PortalPlayer and user interfaces

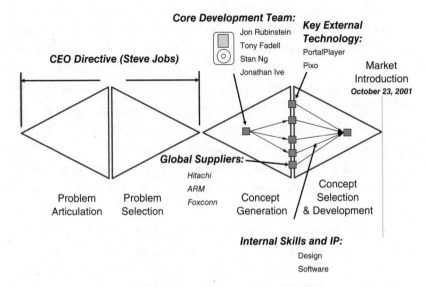

Figure 7.1: Conceptualization of the network innovation process model noting an example of Apple's iPod. © 2016 Tucker J. Marion, Sebastian K. Fixson

from Pixo. In less than 12 months, the design was refined with input from the virtual team, suppliers, and feedback from testing of prototypes.[10] A schematic of Apple's network mode innovation process model is shown in Figure 7.1.

Apple's manufacturing partner, Foxconn, was also a key player in the development and launch of the product, and in the quick retooling for its successive generations. iPod was launched in October 2001 and, by 2007, accounted for a third of Apple's revenue.

Since iPod's introduction, Apple continued to develop and refine its network, moving from being a specialist to having its anchor mode be the network. The iPhone and iPad products were developed using the network, which now includes third-party developers and peripheral accessory companies. The network is all-important to

Apple, from component suppliers to manufacturing. These all have a vested interest in getting the product to market successfully. Foxconn jumped through enormous hoops to change the original iPhone screen from plastic to glass.[11] A simple yet effective phrase indicated Apple's shift to the network mode in the early 2000s. From the first iPod onward, all Apple products state their California design and assembly location. Apple continues to tout its network, even as it shifts some products back to the United States. In advertising their new Mac Pro, they state, "With the new Mac Pro, we assemble the entire product and machine several of its high-precision components in the United States. By leveraging the innovative power of industry-leading companies in Texas, Florida, Illinois, Kentucky, and over a dozen other states across America, we're able to build a product that's impeccably constructed and beautiful in every detail. In other words, exactly as it was envisioned by our designers and engineers in California."[12] Recent reports suggest that Apple has instructed its manufacturing partners Foxconn and Pegatron to investigate manufacturing iPhones in the United States.[13] Regardless of assembly location, the important point is the value of the network to Apple's current and future operations.

Overall, this mode combines a general requirement for substantial product design expertise with sharing behavior typical in networks, both social and vendor. Trust, collaboration, and sharing are key aspects. This mode is not just about transactional supplier relationships but about the development of a sustained ecosystem sharing in a virtuous cycle of innovation. Requirements for performance are high, and the integration of a distributed network of partners from new ventures to large suppliers can be challenging. Until recently, with the exception of firms like Apple, Airbus, and Boeing, this has been the most uncharted of the modes. For innovation executives, the network mode – like the community mode – is an attractive area to explore and an area into which some leading firms like Apple have moved. Like the community mode, this mode is dynamic, with many within the respective spaces experimenting with new business models, trying new approaches to development processes, and addressing risks and challenges.

Level 1: Mode Foundations

Resource Control
The Boeing 777 developed in the 1990s was *the* engineering case study at the time, and it still is a gold standard for successful product development. Boeing's first use of completely digital design and their interaction with suppliers and customers on design decisions were really the culmination of a development mindset led by a co-located, cross-functional team. And it showed in overall project deliverables like on target for cost and for time. But the 777 is not an isolated case. From Team Taurus in the 1980s to the 2011 Chevy Volt, examples are plentiful. And research finds that in this type of development, anchored by cross-functional teams, the best-performing firms use multiple organizational processes relating to team effectiveness and cross-functional cooperation.[14] Fast-forward 10 years to the early 2000s. As firms began to explore the burgeoning potential of outsourcing and offshoring, large firms developing complex systems also took note. And the two forces of digital design and collaborative culture were driving the change.

When Boeing decided to build the 787 Dreamliner, they tried a completely new approach, and the lessons they learned have great importance for those in or transforming into a network mode. The previous model, the 777, was sourced the way every Boeing airliner had been since the 1950s. Most major subsystems were designed and sourced in-house. Save the engines and avionics, wings, fairings, and doors were all done in-house. In contrast, for this new plane, Boeing would rely on its vendors to supply *and* design the parts. And expectations were high. According to *Forbes* magazine, "Boeing enthusiastically embraced outsourcing, both locally and internationally, as a way of lowering costs and accelerating development. The approach was intended to 'reduce the 787's development time from six to four years and development cost from $10 to $6 billion.'"[15] But an all-new airliner is not an office stapler.

Unfortunately, the opposite happened. The plane was ultimately billions over budget and years behind schedule. A Boeing manufacturing manager told us, "We went too far, and would not develop (a new plane) in that fashion again." The transfer of design and manufacturing control of major subsystems caused major problems during development. Parts out of specification, misaligned assembly locations – all amount to substantial issues in a project as complex as an airliner. Similar issues were seen in the development of Airbus's A380.[16]

In the network mode, coordination and control are incredibly important. In the Boeing case, they opted for less control. And taken to the extreme, these outside resources in the network can be used on an intermittent basis, moving past cross-functionality into a new paradigm that minimizes team interaction and selectively engages members only when needed for a specific task. The two forces allow this, but managers need to maintain discipline.[17] The intermittent arrangement in the network mode and its development overtime are shown in Figure 7.2.

The coordination of these resources becomes an all-important issue.[18] In our research, we found that the use of better tools is not necessarily of critical importance.[19] Slack and Yammer and wikis are great, but they will not help your team better control these resources. Communication precision about these resources is essential. We

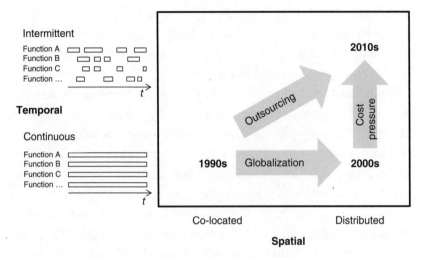

Figure 7.2: Progression to intermittent resource use that characterizes
the network mode.
Source: Tucker J. Marion and Sebastian K. Fixson, "Factors Affecting the
Use of Outside, Intermittent Resources during NPD," *International Journal
of Innovation Science* 6, no. 1 (2014): 1–18.

are in a world where short texts, messages, and posts are the norm.
However, for innovation projects we have found that the communication volume driven by these new tools is not helpful. Less, more
detailed, and precise communication is needed by the team. In our
research, we found that an effective manager's communications
were extremely pointed and direct in communicating design and
project issues. "The hole for the mounting bracket needs to be
here … the thickness of that part needs to be 0.06," and so forth. This
is opposed to more voluminous, ambiguous posts and emails that
are just communication and have little substance. We have found
that the more effective project managers have less email volume,
use the phone more, and rely more on collaborative software like

video and wikis.[20] This is especially important when coordinating multiple suppliers, vendors, and partners in the network. To effectively manage these resources in the network mode, project management training is all-important.

For ground-level project management of the network, brokering individuals provide direction and coordination of the team and project tasks. These virtual resources and organizations may interface with one another, but the primary modes of communication exist between the project leader and the virtual resources. For this project-level function, we define the term "project coordinator" (PC).[21]

Ideally, firms and their PC could select and integrate particular skills at optimal points in the development process. This "plug and play" aspect could reduce fixed team costs and would allow management to direct with pinpoint precision where skilled assets can be deployed with the greatest impact. For example, industrial designers may be tasked with several discrete functions during the project, such as (1) up-front ethnographic research, (2) developing several concepts that express the research findings, and (3) evaluating design progress during detailed design. This may reduce design man-hours substantially versus having an industrial designer on the project full-time from beginning to end. For the project, design is still being performed but in a more targeted, discrete fashion.[22] Apple uses individuals called directly responsible individuals (DRIs) for project management and coordination of these resource issues. The DRI is an Apple best practice and very ingrained in the culture.[23]

Intellectual Property

IP in the network mode can be complex, particularly if you rely on outside partners to be involved in the innovation. In the extreme, you can open your IP to enhance development of the innovation. Tesla has pursued this approach (after developing a suite of patents and establishing itself in a leadership position in a burgeoning market).[24] A company can also take a controlled open-source approach, where the core innovation is available to outside communities but there are still defined rules of engagement for changing the core technology. This is an example of Alphabet's Android operating system. On the other end of the spectrum is a company like Apple, which maintains very tight control of IP and only shares critical design parameters and specifications with their network. Sometimes, suppliers are competitors, as in the case of Apple and Samsung. The lawsuits between these two firms have been in the news for almost a decade. Overall, careful consideration needs to be put into IP strategy to enhance the networks' ability to innovate and reduce constraints. As you explore the network mode, your IP approach is an important up-front planning activity.

Level 2: Organizational Development

Organizational Design

The network mode intensifies the coordination of resources because, in essence, the network mode is characterized by the knitting together these contributors for the joint innovation effort. These resources are temporally, geographically, organizationally, and/or culturally dispersed, but yet they have to act interdependently, often through technology, to achieve a common goal. The team members may differ in their kind, position, discipline, and competencies, and their membership may be temporary according to the needs of the project.[25] This creates inherent challenges for the organization and how it approaches team design. In the case of Boeing's 787 program, on-site Boeing representatives at suppliers were not used.[26] Despite internal Boeing employees noting the importance of supplier management,[27] it was not until after the program experienced severe issues that Boeing deployed engineers to its network. As we have discussed, the coordination of resources is essential. This means having strong project management through a PC at the head of the team because the network is a messy web of actors and interactions. For organizations pursuing this approach, the PC needs authority over the network, and the team needs to have the ability to resemble a traditional cross-functional team when needed. This flexible, tightly controlled team arrangement, when combined with precise communication, is a recipe for success in the network mode.

Task Allocation

As we explored the community mode in chapter 5, there is a great deal of interest and potential benefit from crossing the firm boundary and getting innovation input from the outside. For the community mode, a large collection of enthusiastic and engaged customers can create value. This value is typically a large amount of resources applied collectively to a single problem or a series of problems. For the network mode, you have outside expertise working on various problems, from different vantage points – really a collection of specialists adding to the project. Research has shown that, increasingly, innovation comes from suppliers.[28] A key differentiator between the community mode and the network mode are the forms of coordination with and control over these outside contributors. The outside knowledge creators may be traditional component suppliers, manufacturers, design consultancies, universities, government agencies, individual experts, and even competitors. These relationships tend to follow a continuum, from pure transactional relationships to deep alliances.[29] There are two critical aspects to the network mode: (1) selecting the right actors and (2) coordinating their efforts. And as innovation becomes more distributed, the relationships between the firm and these external innovators become more important. The firm with the better

network wins. That's one of the reasons why GE relocated its headquarters to Boston. With the highest concentration of colleges and
universities in the world, leading venture firms, a thriving and diverse start-up culture, and an educated workforce, Boston is a perfect
fit for a firm looking to enhance its network mode. And this is not just
for large multinationals. Small firms can get an even bigger bang for
their buck from the network mode. Here's an example.

PaperPro was founded in 2003[30] with the launch of a new office
stapler. Their series of products was based upon a proprietary technology invented by a tool design expert in California. Their network
then grew to include a manufacturer in China that could quickly go
from concept to production and help with packaging and fulfillment. PaperPro's products were soon quickly selling off the shelves
of Staples and Office Depot. When looking to enhance their product
line with new variants, they decided to expand their network, this
time with the help of an outside design consultancy. In developing a
new high-capacity stapler, PaperPro contracted a product development firm located outside of Philadelphia, Pennsylvania. During
the initial design phases, the core team (including a product manager) would meet weekly and communicate daily using email. Both
PaperPro and the outside design team fully embraced the two forces.
For design and CAD, all part files were stored on PaperPro's shared
file transfer protocol (FTP) site (the only thing close to a shared cloud
drive or Dropbox at the time), allowing all team members to view
the files remotely. The 3D CAD was done in several locations across
the United States. Since the development was completely distributed, the importance of the FTP site was substantial, though today this
can be done much more effectively using the latest CAD software,
such as Onshape, which is a fully cloud-based design solution.[31]

Rapid prototypes constructed for testing and design validation
were produced by a highly experienced rapid prototype vendor in

Pennsylvania and at the final manufacturer in China. Three series of prototypes were developed before the production tools were initiated in China. Rapid prototypes included machined parts, stamped parts, and 3D-printed parts of various types. The team used the latest additive-manufacturing technology and quick-turn tooling available at the time. All communication with rapid prototype vendors was done via phone and email transmission of part files. PaperPro's core development team communicated with their manufacturer in China using web messaging via Skype.[32] They used instant messaging as well as video to resolve manufacturing issues. New information technology like Teamwork or Slack would have made the process even more efficient.

Core team members leveraged the time zone differences and typically checked email messages well into the evening of US Eastern Standard Time. This allowed very fast resolution of tool and production issues.

The only internal contact during development of PaperPro's new product line was one of the founders; as such the entire development team was virtual. This included engineering, manufacturing, industrial design, prototype, and component vendors. At no time during development did the entire team meet in person. PaperPro's contracted development firm also used a limited development process. This was integrated into PaperPro's very open development paradigm, where no formal process was employed. However, management decision meetings were held throughout the project based on project milestones.[33]

In total, PaperPro's non-recurring engineering (NRE) cost for the project was approximately $125,000. This included contract and internal engineering, as well as the cost of prototypes and testing. One important factor pointing to the benefit of the network was that the cost of development was approximately equal to that of hiring one experienced engineer, while the total amount of actual person hours on the project contributed by the network was far greater than one engineer could perform alone. These actual hours include both charged person hours and in-kind "sweat equity." Our estimates suggest that the total NRE was 50 percent less than a larger, more well-known design firm would cost. PaperPro purchased tooling for high-volume production in China. Because of their network alliance, the manufacturer amortized the cost of the tooling, in essence providing valuable credit to the firm. So the right network partners can be a very good value from a design and manufacturing cost standpoint. The product was developed from concept to tooling kick-off in 14 months. This included three rounds of prototype testing with components made in China and the United States. PaperPro's network mode innovation process framework is shown in Figure 7.3.[34]

Throughout the development process, PaperPro leveraged and developed their network for innovation. The design firm of course led the project and contributed many solid design and engineering decisions to realize the product. However, the manufacturer also provided key insights and design changes, as did the original inventor of the tool technology. A large research university was also engaged during the process, resulting in several studies of components and product platforms, sourcing decision evaluation, and implementation of a product development process. This web of resources contributed greatly to final product performance, as well as to development speed and cost. Recent research notes the importance of suppliers as drivers of innovation.[35] This is why firms operating in the network mode develop such close relationships, as they are essential to transformative innovation. Just look at Tesla's relationship with Panasonic as a prime example. John Deere's deep, long-term relationship with BMW's Designworks design arm is another.[36] In China,

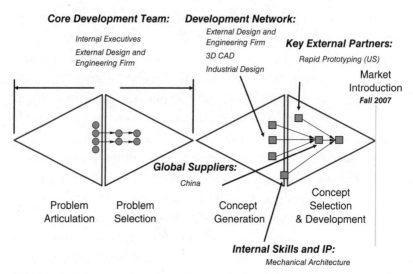

Figure 7.3: PaperPro network mode innovation flow.
© 2016 Tucker J. Marion, Sebastian K. Fixson

Haier has developed an ecosystem of problem-solvers, which in-clude large companies such as Dow Chemical and Honeywell as well as individuals. Currently, approximately 30 firms pay to use this innovation ecosystem. Along the same lines, Lenovo has devel-oped an online platform to foster collaboration with start-ups.[37]

We noted earlier two essential aspects of the network mode: selecting the right partners and coordinating them. In the case of PaperPro, the original company was extremely fortunate to find the right technical partner, an expert inventor who put them in touch with a reputable and very capable manufacturer that hap-pened to assist in prototyping, shipping, and fulfillment. Each of these was found via networking the traditional way and by word of mouth, and ultimately selected because there was a good per-sonal fit between parties. Research has shown that a large amount of trust can be built between the parties, eventually leading to strong alliances that go far beyond traditional transactional relationships.[38] With PaperPro's foray into the network mode, after a brief period of getting to know each other, parties began to build trust with one another, leading to verification through results (hitting milestones early, better than expected working prototypes, high-quality initial production samples, introduction to sales personnel, etc.). In the case of their line extensions, the third-party design consultancy was recommended though personal contacts of one of the founders, and although this relationship was more transactional, it remained one of mutual trust and joint admiration. In terms of coordination, PaperPro's development efforts were always led by an experienced project manager, or project coordinator. This is the same as seen at Apple, with the iPod as a prime example.

In a study of successful ventures and research used to inform this book, we noticed commonalities in the development and selection of their network. First, using outside resources to drive innovation was at the core of these firms' innovation strategy. And in selecting these partners, they sought ones that complemented their skills and also enhanced their strategic mission. Research has also shown that you need to select partners that mesh well with the various cultures and management style involved.[39] Last, when developing the network, don't overlook the individual. High-impact individuals and experts can have a huge impact on a project. One of the firms we researched found that an older software engineer was the key aspect in developing a class-leading firmware solution for an IoT device. An internal team would have taken months or years to develop as good a solution. And he was a freelancer who lived in Oregon and interfaced with the team by phone and email. This individual was found via word of mouth as well.

The web of resources in the network ecosystem goes well beyond the list of component suppliers and manufacturers. As described so far in this chapter, both Apple and PaperPro used small ventures and start-ups for key pieces of the innovation puzzle. This is important, as new ventures can be a source of new technology, an entrepreneurial mindset and culture, and potential targets for acquisition. In selecting new network partners, as a larger firm, *do not* shy away from small or new ventures. While there is a risk, often it is overshadowed by the entrepreneurial spirit and grit a hungry small company can bring to the table. Don't base decisions on size and age alone. The question is where to find new ventures. Though the total number of new venture starts is at its lowest level in decades, recent research suggests the source for great new ventures has spread from the typical centers of Boston, San Francisco, and New York.[40] Austin, Philadelphia, Salt Lake City, Los Angeles, and North Carolina are seeing surges in new venture development. Many of these resources can be found in existing communities near firm headquarters, divisions, and manufacturing centers.

A 2016 article in *The Atlantic* chronicled an investigation in how the United States is putting itself back together from the bottom up, a rebirth driven by communities.[41] A key finding in the article was the role universities play in this process. Universities are an important aspect of the network mode. Since the end of World War II, universities have been the engine of basic research, research that has formed the basis of major technological innovations. From the internet to biotechnology, universities are at the front line of technology research and invention. In essence, universities have replaced corporate exploratory R&D. In such an environment, firms need to develop stronger ties with universities, and sponsored research is one path to explore. One study of technology transfer efficacy found that seeking entrepreneurial faculty, combined with company-sponsored applied research (research that has an application, not basic research which can take decades to reach the market), results in spin-outs and an increased chance of licensing the technology to outside firms.[42] Executives need to reach out, find entrepreneurially inclined science and business faculty, and develop sustained engagement. As mentioned, firms like GE are in the process of doing this. GE's move to Boston was in part driven by proximity to top universities. During the planning and selection process, GE had meetings with all the major research universities in the Boston area to discuss research, collaboration, and talent development. As you explore this mode, think about ways you can engage with local universities near your major centers of R&D and manufacturing.

Overall, the selection of network members is important. Firms in the network start to move beyond pure transactional arrangement to form deep alliances and partnerships. During inevitable crisis moments, the network members can become extremely close. Research has shown that deep bonds form between members.[43] In developing the network, it is important to think beyond traditional evaluation criteria like cost and capability. These are important, of course, but innovation can be messy, and consideration needs to be given to the individuals or firms that will bend over backward to help realize an innovation. In the example of PaperPro we discussed earlier, the vendor in China was very good, but their ability to go the "extra mile" proved their worth to the project and was essential to the positive outcome of the first and successive projects. And in several cases, they continued to innovate and provide interesting design alternatives that were not directed from the design team. They just did it. And they didn't charge for it. In many cases these innovations ended up being critical to the performance and cost performance of the final product. Firms looking to enhance or enter this mode must give suppliers and vendors the room for innovation. You need control and coordination, but increasing the "slack" of management and the purse strings can pay dividends.

Level 3: Implementation

Incentives
Firms operating in the network mode share in the innovation process efforts and should also share in its success. While joint ventures and partnerships are well trod, joint incentive systems for success should be considered. They may include ownership sharing, profit and revenue sharing, and other joint mechanisms to share in the potential and success of the innovation. As you consider incentives, aligning interests, transparency, and prudent contract design are essential.[44]

New KPIs
In this mode, the network ecosystem is increasingly responsible for innovation. From key components to operating systems, these actors have substantial control over innovation outcomes. For the network mode to function properly, the controlling firm needs to move beyond metrics like cost, schedule, performance to specifications, and quality. In this tightly knit ecosystem, joint training skill metrics, communication quantity and quality, and team enthusiasm need to be considered. Just look at Toyota and their joint training and relationship building.[45] Their supplier interaction has moved beyond the original keiretsu concept and is a model of relationship building within the network.

Summary

The network mode is dynamic and increasingly important to innovation. Who is in the network, how it is arranged, and how well it is managed are critical to the success of efforts in this mode. We have seen what happens when it goes wrong but also when it goes right. And when it goes well, it can be transformative. For executives, the network mode is a natural progression from the specialist mode; it spreads and enhances the locus of innovation and creates a web of resources that can be vital to staying a step ahead of the competition. Firms with the best network, and the best-managed network mode, win.

Key Points

- The network mode is not just a collection of vendors but an ecosystem of partnerships that spans start-ups to research universities.
- The network mode is a natural progression from the specialist mode, with an increased focus on core competencies. But this does not mean eliminating all vertical integration.
- Selection of the right network partners is vital.
- The network can spread and enhance where innovation comes from, but this needs to be managed prudently. Going too far too fast is a concern.
- New ventures and universities can be key partners in this mode. And consider inroads into local offices and centers, rather than just the headquarters.
- Intellectual property and incentives for the network need to be carefully considered, and these also present an opportunity to do things differently.

Assessments

Here are questions you and your team should ask as you explore and develop your network mode:

- What do you consider to be your core competency as a company?
- Who are your current key vendors and partners?
- How is your relationship with these key vendors? Transactional or something more?
- How much input do these vendors have into the innovation process?
- Do you have any relationships with start-ups? Are any key technologies sourced from them?
- Do you have any current research initiatives with universities? Are they sponsored research for an application?
- Do you co-develop or share IP with your vendors?
- Do you encourage IP development with your partners?
- Are any technologies open for your vendor community to share or co-contribute?
- In managing vendors, partners, and resources during projects, what level of control or coordination do you have?
- What role does technology play in facilitating network coordination?
- Do you have Apple-like DRIs or heavyweight PCs?

For More Information

Here are additional materials that explore the network mode and issues with managing innovation ecosystems and external partners:

Aoki, Katsuki, and Thomas Taro Lennerfors. "The New Improved Keiretsu." *Harvard Business Review*, September 2013. https://hbr.org/2013/09/the -new-improved-keiretsu.

Henke, John W. Jr., and Chun Zhang. "Increasing Supplier-Driven Innovation." *MIT Sloan Management Review* 51, no. 2 (2010). https://sloanreview.mit.edu /article/increasing-supplier-driven-innovation/.

Marion, Tucker J., and Sebastian K. Fixson. "Factors Affecting the Use of Outside, Intermittent Resources during NPD." *International Journal of Innovation Science* 6, no. 1 (2014): 1–18.

Marion, Tucker J., Kim A. Eddleston, John H. Friar, and David Deeds. "The Evolution of Interorganizational Relationships in Emerging Ventures: An Ethnographic Study within the New Product Development Process." *Journal of Business Venturing* 30, no. 1 (2015): 167–84.

The Multimode Organization

In this book, we have discussed that because of the two forces, the innovation landscape is now larger and more diverse. This allows specialists to develop new, revolutionary designs more quickly. It enables motivated individuals, deep within the corporate walls, to enact change through a new venture. Networks of service providers foster innovation ecosystems, where the sources of innovation expand well beyond traditional supply chains. And finally, easy interaction with large numbers of customers, users, and enthusiasts creates new opportunities for knowledge creation. For the company, this creates both opportunities and challenges. How do you leverage new modes, and can you play in all modes at once? What are the trade-offs? And how does that look from an organizational and resource perspective? This chapter sheds light on what it takes to become a multimode organization.

In the previous chapters we spent time detailing the intricacies of the four modes. The discussion of the modes individually is important, as each mode is characterized by its own set of opportunities and challenges. Each mode also exposes differences in the interactions with customers, suppliers, and other partners. As a consequence, each mode requires its own managerial logic. For example, the specialist mode demands an internal incentive system, promotion rules, and organizational culture that values capability development. In contrast, an organization active in the community mode must build relationships with a large, distributed community, encouraging engagement through both monetary and non-monetary incentive mechanisms. This in turn has consequences for the internal culture, which needs to be open-minded to input and suggestions from outside the company; it must not exhibit a "not-invented-here" syndrome. In summary, the first order of business for managers is to create an alignment between their internal structures and the innovation modes in which their organizations engage. For this reason, we focused each chapter on the Six Factors to give executives a pertinent framework for each mode.

Since the innovation landscape has increased in size and diversity, managers might decide to pursue different opportunities with different innovation modes, exploring and exploiting multiple modes simultaneously. Larger firms especially might decide to invest resources to explore adjacent innovation modes. Consider the case of GE that we discussed in chapter 3, with experiments ranging from GE Garages (venture mode) to FirstBuild (community mode) in their appliance division (now part of Haier Group). These are examples of a specialist "testing the waters" of other modes and adding value to their business units. In the case of GE Appliances, their embrace of the venture and community modes contributed to the successful sale of the division.[1] Many specialist firms are exploring the community mode, without having to adjust their entire internal structure and processes toward this mode of working at once. Examples include P&G, Airbus, and Hasbro. More generally, firms can experiment or try test cases to leverage the unique benefits of other modes, such as the venture, community, or network mode. As the innovation landscape expands, the need for firms to become adept at being multimodal will be increasingly important. This goes beyond the ability to be ambidextrous and being skilled at exploring and exploiting internal resources. It is what will separate highly successful companies from the rest over the next decade and beyond.

Let's return to our four-modes framework, first introduced in chapter 3. Figure 8.1 shows the framework with the expected distributions added. As we discussed, along the horizontal axis we define the organizational scope of the framework. For example, the community scope is external, while on the left side of the axis are those projects that predominantly rely on internal resources, such as employee-centric new ventures and general R&D. Along the vertical axis of the framework is a range of incentive mechanisms, separated by the degree of formality.

The structure and balance of the incentives and the organizational scope form the map of the landscape. And as we have seen, each of the modes has a distinct DNA as it relates to the Six Factors. Regardless of which mode is your "anchor," you need to step back and view this landscape from a high level to see the common thread that runs through each mode and where each can fit into the overall innovation structure of your firm.

Taking a Step Back: The Overall Picture

There are many definitions of innovation. But typically the definition includes terms such as "new," "ideas," "transformational," and so on. And frankly, it is overused in the same vein as "disruption." But for the executive at a for-profit firm, innovation usually means *new products or services that increase revenue, drive growth in net profits, and distinguish your offerings from the competition*. It's a goal as simple as that. To accomplish this objective, there is a process through which resources are committed to a project and are managed to various degrees of effectiveness, and whose final project form has enough

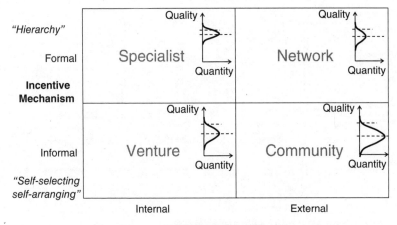

Figure 8.1: Innovation mode framework.
© 2018 Tucker J. Marion, Sebastian K. Fixson

value to accomplish the overall goal. All firms have an innovation process, some more explicit, some more ad hoc. To discuss what is happening in innovation activities, let's again take a look at a generic innovation process (Figure 8.2).

Once an opportunity arises, firms commit resources to articulate the problem to be solved and generate ideas, some of which are ultimately selected. The same process is done for concept generation, selection, and development. At the core, fundamental to the business is getting the best idea through that process to market commercialization. Three factors are needed to accomplish this: (1) generating an abundance of ideas based on good opportunities; (2) generating ideas that are of high quality; and (3) selecting the best ideas to move forward with development. Easy, right? Well, remember, new product and service failure rates haven't changed much since the 1960s, hovering around 40 percent.[2] For every iPod,

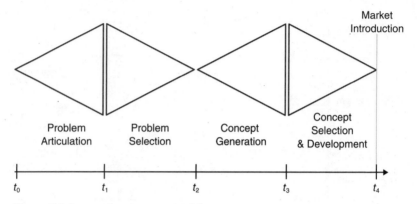

Figure 8.2: Innovation process model.
© 2016 Tucker J. Marion, Sebastian K. Fixson

there is a Microsoft Zune. At its essence, the new expanded innovation landscape offers firms different ways to tweak and tinker
with those three factors. Each mode promises different results,
which, depending on the company's needs, may fit into different
places in the process. So let's dive into the overall process.

A Multimode Innovation Process

To better ground our insights, we introduced the innovation process
framework, which considers the problem space and the solution
space separately within the overall innovation process (shown in
Figure 8.3). Various forms of innovation via the modes can be located in the framework. For example, an innovation contest organized by an intermediary such as InnoCentive sits squarely in the
solution space (the right side of Figure 8.3). It begins with a well-
articulated problem and invites solution options, from which a winner is selected. On the other hand, when a company asks its customer

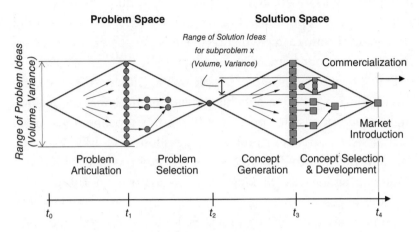

Figure 8.3: Innovation process framework, parsed showing ideas and solutions. © 2016 Tucker J. Marion, Sebastian K. Fixson

base for ideas for new products, it essentially searches the *problem space* (the left side of Figure 8.3).

In chapter 6 we discussed the company Quirky in detail. Quirky's process was unique in that it engaged its community members on both sides, albeit in different forms, and its model combined elements of both competition and collaboration. In an ongoing process, every member could submit ideas (i.e., "problems" in our framework). From this idea pool, a small number were selected through a two-phase process. First, once ideas were posted, the community commented on them, sometimes combined them, and ultimately rated them on a point system. Those ideas that floated to the top then entered the second step: an evaluation at which a combination of management and community made the final selection decision. Once the company had selected a problem to work on, it broke down the actual product development work into a number of mini-contests on concept designs, naming possibilities, and design issues. The community was invited to participate in these mini-contests, incentivized by the opportunity to earn influence points, which could later translate into cash payments (this work is positioned in the solution space in our framework, highlighted by the orange boxes).

Engaging a broad group of people or stakeholders (i.e., the community) brings with it a possible pipeline of ideas that can include high-value options. To continue refilling this pipeline – that is, to keep a steady stream of problem suggestions – Quirky made the inherent promise to produce as many of the products as it could (Quirky's tagline was "Making invention accessible"). This promise tied the hopes of inventors, the community, and customers to a stream of new and exciting products. Both the inventor and community were compensated, with the inventor given a generous royalty and the community contributors paid via a sophisticated, albeit in its details somewhat opaque, incentive system.[3] Consequently, both of these outside actors had a vested interest in seeing their ideas get to market. This produced a condition where there was a lack of constraint in the *problem space* and a commitment constraint in the *solution space*. While volume of ideas is a benefit of open innovation, Quirky was completely reliant on the community for all ideas and concepts. And because Quirky was tied to both the inventor and the community in terms of incentives and commitments to develop, their portfolio management was tied to the promise of commercializing as many of the community's ideas as possible.

Overall, individuals involved in the process can be very fast in the innovation contest format, but project speed might come into conflict with the expectations of stakeholders in other portions of the innovation process, particularly when decisions need to be made efficiently from design finalization through first sale. Quirky tried to rely on the community on both sides of the process. This proved untenable and was a factor in their bankruptcy. For firms becoming multimodal, you need to know when and where in the process to deploy each mode to its greatest effectiveness. Sometimes deployment can be sequential, other times in parallel.

In looking at the overall process we know the strengths and weaknesses of each mode. The community mode and open innovation in general can generate a lot of ideas. However, as we have seen with Quirky, the average quality of the ideas may be lacking. Incentives help, though these alone do not guarantee the best ideas. But these efforts can be cost-effective. Specialists can be highly successful in the quality of ideas and solutions, but the quantity can be limited by the general nature of the resources at hand. And quality R&D is expensive. Though internal ventures may increase the number of ideas, the quality may not be as high as with experts in the company. However, experimenting using lean start-up methods can be very cost-effective. And finally, the network may increase quantity of ideas over experts, but quality can be unpredictable based on the expertise of the network. The network can also be cost- and time-efficient. Of course, different approaches can be taken in each mode. These initiatives can have very different characteristics regarding the quantity, quality, and use of resources (both cost and impact on the organization) to generate ideas and knowledge. In Table 8.1, several example approaches are listed for each mode.

In overlaying the pros of each mode, the approaches you might use within the overall process can help direct your overall strategy for becoming a multimode organization. This is shown in Figure 8.4, which shows the innovation mode framework together with the innovation process framework. This multimode use is an example of a sequential deployment during the innovation process.

Multimode organizations can use each mode effectively in different parts of the process, leveraging their inherent strengths without being tied to their disadvantages throughout the entire process. As we mentioned earlier, these can be deployed sequentially or in parallel. Here's an example of sequential use of multiple modes during the

Table 8.1. Example approaches and initiatives in each mode

Mode	Example Approaches	Idea/Knowledge Specifics		
		Quantity	Quality	Resource Use
Specialist	Develop a pure project "skunkworks" team	Low	High	High
	Initiate internal ideation boot camps	Medium	Medium	Low
	Hire highly skilled industry experts where appropriate	Low	High	High
Network	Engage with design innovation consultancies	Low	High	High
	Engage with outside technology firms and suppliers	Medium	High	High
	Establish an applied research lab with a research university	Low	Medium	Medium
Community	Develop a social strategy on social media to inform innovation	High	Low	Low
	Develop a custom digital platform to connect users and internal resources	High	Medium	Medium
	Incentivize contests and hack-a-thons	High	Medium	Low
Venture	Establish "free time" rules to pursue personal projects	Low	Medium	Low
	Establish an incentivized system for internal idea generation	Medium	Medium	Medium
	Develop a funded new venture network and ecosystem	Medium	High	Medium

innovation process (illustrated in the bottom portion of Figure 8.4). Let's say the C-suite wants to engage with customers in a new, untested market. Budgets are tight, and this is really an exploration. You might run an innovation contest to generate a lot of ideas (C: community). Some of the ideas might be interesting, so you employ your R&D team to vet and select, combining if appropriate (S: specialist).

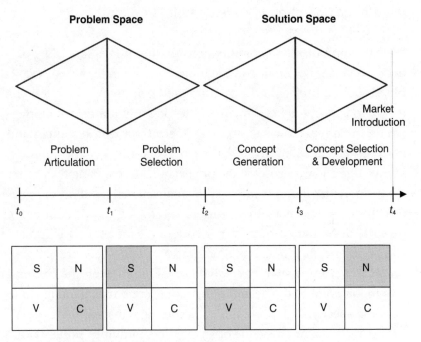

Figure 8.4: Innovation process model and mode frameworks.
© 2016 Tucker J. Marion, Sebastian K. Fixson

Once the opportunity is identified, internally you might have a conceptual contest among your employees (V: venture). To develop the idea cost-effectively, this new venture may tap into the network to develop the concept for a limited market test (N: network). In this simple example, the firm uses each mode where it can be the most impactful, from the perspective of knowledge creation, cost, and speed. Not all cases are alike, so you must be flexible and adaptable in your adoption of multiple modes. Modes are also dynamic, so this needs to be considered. Multimode use can be separated into three operating conditions. The first is the use of modes in combinations.

Multimode Condition 1: Mode Combinations

We can think of mode combinations as the innovation DNA of a firm. There are base pair combinations that naturally fit. For example, starting a project in the venture mode, applying lean methods for rapid concept development and testing, can jumpstart an innovation initiative. However, to make the project real, resources and partners are needed. To lower fixed costs and get the required knowledge and expertise on the project quickly, realizing the project via the network mode makes sense. We discussed the iPod in previous chapters. This is really a story of leveraging the venture mode for early development and the network mode for final development and commercialization. The iPod was a venture-network pairing. The many examples we have given of GE employing the community mode point to the benefit of using the community mode along with the specialist mode. It is also becoming apparent that specialists are recognizing the value of an expert community, rather than a community of laypeople. This is particularly true with more complex engineering projects. The joint GE and Quirky experiment with appliances showed the limits of general community involvement. In one interview with management who were involved, the following was noted: "There were poor technology choices and GE pushed very hard." Ultimately the real design and engineering decisions were made by the internal design team, bypassing the general community entirely. In contrast, GE's interaction with GrabCAD and the design of a bracket with input from a community of higher levels of expertise was much different. A person involved in the project said, "Many people at GE thought it was a bad idea, but ultimately were proven wrong."

The network and community modes also can work well together, particularly in situations where an expert community is a valued part of the network. We see these expert communities in firms like InnoCentive. The restarted Quirky 2.0 is also offering partnerships with existing firms. An example of the network and community modes working together is at one large computer manufacturer. Over the last 15 years, the division has established an active user community that contributes insights into next-generation features and specifications. The community interacts with each other on a custom web-based platform run by the R&D team. Questions about upcoming features are facilitated by the R&D team, and these are ultimately translated into a running detailed specification sheet for the next series of designs. The community is extremely close-knit. Every year the company holds a week-long conference at its head-quarters. And it's not just a sales meeting. Community members bring their families, and strong bonds have formed even between competitors. One of the R&D team members noted that the conference is the highlight of the year for those who attend.

Last, the combination of the specialist mode and the network mode are a natural pairing. Many firms take advantage of the network's benefit of an innovation ecosystem. Take Autodesk, which is building relationships with start-ups like Hackrod, a new venture developing 3D-printed vehicle platforms.[4] They are partnering with universities and the community with their BUILD! space in Boston, Massachusetts. Autodesk University is building network relationships and educational opportunities. The specialist and network modes can bring together unlikely partnerships. GM and Ford recently collaborated on a new 10-speed automatic transmission.[5] These are the fiercest of competitors, but the network and specialist mode combination offers tangible performance improvements. The combined expertise resulted in a high-performance product with a lower overall cost. The two companies will be able to leverage the transmission platform for different applications and can differentiate them with each firms' different software and gear choices. GM has invested in the ride-sharing company Lyft and has also invested in or acquired new ventures in the autonomous vehicle technology space. The firm started GM Ventures in 2016 and is expanding their network-based innovation ecosystem one piece at a time. In addition, they have launched open innovation centers focused on self-driving vehicle software development.[6]

In looking at adopting a combinatory approach, there are trade-offs to consider. As we have discussed, each mode has strengths and limitations in terms of problem and solution quantity, quality, cost, and risk. These dictate when and where you might consider using a particular mode. For example, in our innovation process model we note that a range of solution ideas can be formulated to solve a problem. Let's say the parameters of the problem are well defined – for example, design input on a new suspension piece for a high-end motorcycle. If you were to use the community mode, a wide-open call to the general public may not be the wisest choice. Yes, you'll get a high quantity of ideas, but the average quality probably will be lower than a targeted campaign using a select community of experts such as Forth by Local Motors, a community-based design consulting initiative. But engaging with a specialized engineering firm may be a better choice, to have higher-quality solutions but lower quantities of them. On the downside, the engineering firm may be more costly than Forth. In managing the mode choice, we can think about the four variables of quantity, quality, cost, and risk as we work to understand and make good trade-off decisions.

To summarize, for the specialist mode, because of resource constraints, the overall quantity of ideas can be low, while the quality can be high. Good resources are costly, but the overall risk is somewhat low. For the venture mode, the quantity of ideas from the internal organization can be quite high (think of innovation contest submissions), while the average quality may not be as high as in the case of subject matter experts. However, these can be very cost-effective and the risk is low. For the network, because of the nature of outside interactions, there may be fewer ideas, but depending upon who is in your innovation ecosystem, the quality can be high. Costs are elevated but still can be lower than the specialist mode (Foxconn can run manufacturing more efficiently than Apple-run factories). Risk for the network is high, as the selection and management of key relationships is important and key innovation is outside of the corporate walls. Lastly, the community can generate a large quantity of ideas, but the quality can be low. Cost is also low, but there is higher risk, as the community may or may not be the source of the best ideas. These trade-offs are shown in Figure 8.5. We give each mode a rating of 1, 3, 6, or 9 for each of the strengths. For example, the community mode is rated a 9 on the quantity scale and a 3 on cost, since attempts to work in the community mode are generally cost-effective for generating knowledge and a lot of ideas.

Given that each mode has its own merits, we can posit which modes make the best combinations and if all combinations are possible. In Figure 8.6, we list notable mode combinations with comments on use and effectiveness.

Certain mode combinations lend themselves to certain phases. As we discussed earlier in the chapter, we segmented the innovation process into two halves: the problem space and the solution space. Both of these phases have unique properties relating to problem articulation and selection, concept generation, selection, and development; so when considering mode combinations, you need to consider when and where these mode combinations fit within each space. For example, if your firm wants to generate a lot of ideas quickly and for low cost, having internal idea contests and external community competitions (venture-community combination) may make a lot of

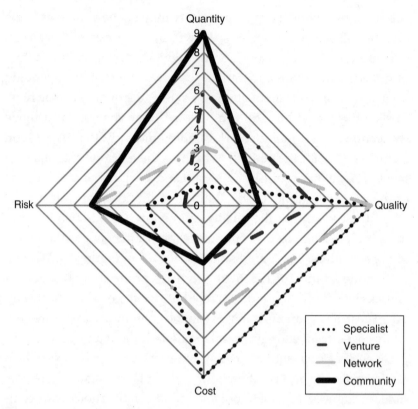

Figure 8.5: Relative mode strengths.

sense in parallel during problem articulation (problem space) or concept generation (solution space). Other combinations work well in each phase sequentially, as we have seen with the specialist-community combination. The Airbus–Local Motors collaboration is an example of such a sequential pairing. We acknowledge that the number of potential combinations in each of the phases can be large, but we believe the suggested combinations shown in Figure 8.6 represent a logical roadmap for adopting a multimode strategy within the process.

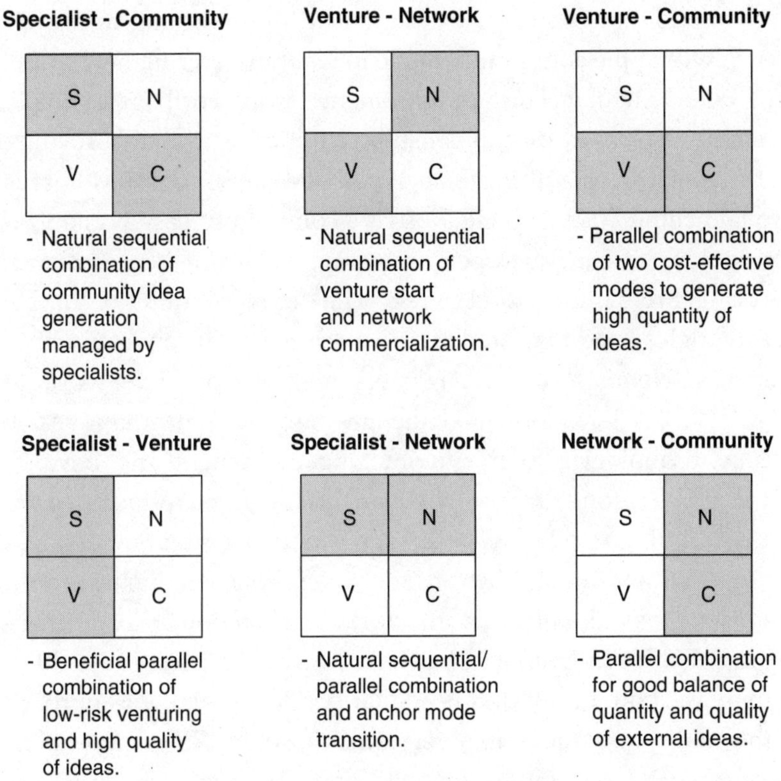

Specialist - Community

S	N
V	C

- Natural sequential combination of community idea generation managed by specialists.

Venture - Network

S	N
V	C

- Natural sequential combination of venture start and network commercialization.

Venture - Community

S	N
V	C

- Parallel combination of two cost-effective modes to generate high quantity of ideas.

Specialist - Venture

S	N
V	C

- Beneficial parallel combination of low-risk venturing and high quality of ideas.

Specialist - Network

S	N
V	C

- Natural sequential/ parallel combination and anchor mode transition.

Network - Community

S	N
V	C

- Parallel combination for good balance of quantity and quality of external ideas.

Figure 8.6: Mode combination examples.

Multimode Condition 2: Mode Dynamics and Transitions

In chapter 3 we discussed several cases where firms modify their approach within a mode and also over time change their dominant mode, which we term their "anchor mode." Apple transitioned from a pure specialist to operating in the network mode. Changes in trade, politics, and management played a crucial role in this transition. The two forces – digital design and collaborative culture – and the constant churn of technology add to the dynamism within a given mode. For example, we see Local Motors changing its approach within the community mode in real time, adding new sources of revenue with its Forth development service. Forth is essentially a community-based design consulting initiative available for hire by firms, many of which are anchored specialists. Local Motors is also launching Fuse with GE. Fuse is a community-based organization looking to combine open innovation with small-batch manufacturing. Press information states, "The digital community for this new model is headquartered at fuse.ge.com, which convenes entrepreneurs, scientists, coders, engineers, makers around the world to solve product development challenges ranging from non-invasive testing technologies to in-situ imaging equipment and beyond. Physical operations for Fuse will come to life in micro-factories designed to bring together GE teams, customers, entrepreneurs, student groups and more. Micro-factory operations will include rapid prototyping, small-batch manufacturing, and modular experimentation."[7] The first micro-factory opened in Chicago in December 2016. In this case, both Local Motors and GE are adjusting their approach in the community mode in a very quick fashion. GE began experimenting with communities and open innovation just a few years ago. One of the first examples was on the bracket design with GrabCAD. This was followed by work with Quirky and by FirstBuild with Local Motors. Now, only a few years later, GE's approach to the community mode is more mature and entrenched within their organization. Their agility, willingness to partner with untested new ventures, and experimental approaches are essential to achieve the dynamics present in these new modes. As firms explore new modes, they need to be receptive to adjusting their approach once within a mode. And sometimes changing strategic priorities allow you to shift back to other modes, as in the case of Apple re-engaging their inner specialist by considering taking microprocessors in-house from Intel. Mode dynamics can be a two-way street. It's important to note that new mode development and experimentation may take time to fully bear fruit. Patience and a long-term view are necessary as you consider multimodality.

Multimode Condition 3: Running Modes in Parallel

The third multimode condition is operating with the modes deployed in parallel. In other words, the organization uses one mode for some projects and another mode for other projects. This situation is the most challenging to manage, as it requires providing conflicting incentives to different stakeholders. For example, in the specialist mode you need to be credible when you ask your employees to become highly developed experts, but if you also work in the community mode, you need your experts to avoid the "not-invented here" syndrome. These situations will create real tensions that need to be managed. But in looking at the overall goal of innovation, at specific points in the problem and solution spaces, parallel operations can make sense. With complex problems, seeking outside expertise from a community might make sense in parallel with internal experts. Let's say you are a biotechnology company looking to investigate the distribution of targeted drugs in a tissue using nanotechnology. Your internal team has hit roadblocks and is not making progress. You might use InnoCentive and sponsor a challenge, offering $50,000 to the winner. The challenge would ask for novel techniques into the manufacture of carbon nanotubes with embedded medication. Contest participants might be research universities, highly skilled individuals, or startups. This is an example of a firm using a parallel specialist-community pairing.

As with the experimentation with and use of any of the modes, using parallel combinations requires an organization that is willing and able to be in "competition" with resources that are typically outside the organization (the community and the network) or potentially outside the R&D group or business unit (the venture). As we mentioned, this can cause tensions, but it is really in the hands of upper-level management to create an innovation climate that can support these initiatives. These include fostering increases in trust, risk taking, and incentives for collaboration. Such growth can take time, especially for a specialist ingrained in internal development bolstered by decades of inertia. In looking at running in parallel modes, an important consideration is training your employees on what is available. How many of your employees are knowledgeable about Forth, InnoCentive, GrabCAD, Kickstarter, and the many others that are representatives of the new modes? A first step in becoming a multimode organization is understanding the landscape, its actors, and how they might be useful to your innovation team. Then you need to have the flexibility to integrate these modes into the organization. This is where the Six Factors come into play. Firms need to have the ability to adjust the mode foundations (resource control, IP), organizational development (organizational design and task allocation), and implementation strategies (incentives and KPIs). This requires giving business units the freedom to control and hone these foundations. This may be a challenge for your firm, but it is the only way to become a true multimode entity.

Summary

In the introduction we mentioned Takeuchi and Nonaka's recommendation that firms replace their old, sequential new product development process with a new approach – rugby-style, passing the "ball" within the team down the field.[8] They called it the "new new product development game." This time, the forces of digital design and a collaborating culture are creating an *expanded* innovation landscape, which encourages many more and farther-reaching changes in how companies conceive, develop, and commercialize new products and services.

In this expanded innovation landscape, four distinct modes are emerging. Each mode comes with different but significant ramifications for all stakeholders and participants in the process, from lead users to C-suite executives. We encourage firms to explore these different modes but to do so with clear expectations and a firm grasp of the risk and reward potential. We believe that the most successful firms navigating this expanded landscape will have the skills to operate effectively in different modes concomitantly and to leverage the benefits of each mode at different points and projects within the innovation process. It's time to get started.

Key Points

- Firms are increasingly experimenting in becoming multimode organizations.
- The innovation process is composed of separate phases, which enable the use of different modes at times when they can be the most effective.
- Beneficial mode pairings can be used in sequential or parallel combination during the innovation process.
- Firms need to have their organization's Six Factors aligned to deploy modes when and where they can positively impact the process.
- Not all mode combinations make sense, but there are logical pairings that can be easily adopted and experimented with.
- Firms need to expose their innovation organizations to the new modes and be trained on how to best leverage the expanded landscape.
- New modes should be iterative and adaptive to change.

- Fully leveraging a multimode strategy may take time; executives need to think beyond the next quarter as they navigate their organization toward multimode operation.

Assessments

As a first step in becoming a multimode organization, you need to evaluate your innovation portfolio and strategy. Please review the following questions with your team, rating them on a scale of 1–5, (1 being "strongly disagree" and 5 being "strongly agree"):

- Do your business units have the ability to independently control resources?
- Do your business units have the ability to change IP strategy?
- Can your business units experiment with organizational and team design?
- Can your business units use KPIs that are different than standard corporate measures?
- Do your directors and project leaders have authority to change task allocation, sourcing partners, etc.?
- Do your directors and project leaders have control over incentives to employees and outside resources?
- Will upper-level management, directors, and shareholders tolerate experimentation in multiple modes that may take time and resources?

If you have earned a score of over 30, then your Six Factors may be primed to leverage multiple modes. If your score is lower than 20, you have work to do. Your mode foundations need improvement. Now, let's consider the following questions:

- Are your employees trained or exposed to the latest technologies and trends of the two forces?

- What is currently your predominant or anchor mode?
- Are venture and community modes of key interest to the C-suite in your firm?
- How much are executives, directors, and innovation employees exposed to examples of the network, venture, and community modes?
- Does your firm encourage and engage in innovation-specific training?
- Are you currently operating in more than one mode? If so, what are the results?
- If you were to try mode combinations in the problem space or solution space, which ones would you choose?
- If you were tasked with immediate mode experimentation now, for zero cost, how would you proceed?
- What external relationships do you need to foster to develop new modes?

For More Information

This short article is a good synopsis for your managers and employees on the modes and benefits of being a multimode organization:

Marion, Tucker J., and Sebastian K. Fixson. "The 4 Main Ways to Innovate in the Digital Economy." *Harvard Business Review*, June 2, 2016. https://hbr .org/2016/06/the-4-main-ways-to-innovate-in-a-digital-economy.

We have also developed a simulation game that explores how different modes can be used to influence idea generation and discusses the pros and cons of each. This simulation is designed to be used for executive training.

Marion, Tucker J., and Sebastian K. Fixson. "Innovation: Breaking News!" *Harvard Business Publishing*, 2017.

Conclusions and Thoughts on the Future

Throughout this book we have discussed how the perfect storm of digital design and a collaborative culture has initiated a second industrial revolution – a revolution that has expanded the innovation landscape and created new modes of innovation. This allows firms to create more opportunities and ideas and to seek ways to solve design problems using actors and contributors in new manners. We are in the beginning stages of seeing how these new modes, when used together during the innovation process, can radically impact the important factors that have always challenged innovation managers: getting the best ideas designed well and commercialized with the least amount of resources. By selectively combining different innovation modes, sequentially and in parallel, firms can have complementary assets deployed when and where needed.

Ambidexterity to simultaneously explore new opportunities while exploiting existing ones has been talked about for years – and academics have produced a long stream of literature about it – but here we are discussing the ability of firms to "mass-customize" their innovation process itself by leveraging new modes. In chapter 1 we discussed the traditional three paradigms of resource control, task allocation, and corporate structure, which naturally arise when an organization develops. For firms seeking to explore new modes, we dove a level deeper and discussed six factors that firms need to consider during mode development and implementation. And in each mode, there are unique differences in how each mode should be developed, managed, and measured. Overall, the organization needs to develop a modular approach to R&D structured processes. And what's important about modularity? Think about Legos. It's all about the interfaces – how the venture is integrated into the network, how the community platform information and knowledge base are integrated into the internal R&D department. Information and knowledge sharing, specifications management, IT and supporting systems, process management, and gated processes should all be designed to have clear and clean lines of engagement to permit the smooth integration of the modes throughout the innovation process.

In addition to mastering specific innovation modes, in the long run companies need to develop the skill to understand the relative advantages between the modes, to develop skills in the relevant mode(s), and then to move from mode to mode as necessary. This type of agility in switching modes is important because while we currently have identified four main modes of innovation, we see entirely new ones emerging on the horizon. For example, one can already see an "AI mode," where the tools have become so advanced that computers provide much of the solution generation process.

In a potential AI mode, the tools themselves are the beginning. For example, under the heading of generative design, Autodesk is developing a whole new suite of tools that can "automatically" rework designs (i.e., create a vast number of solution options and – with some human guidance – automate the selection procedure). This trend will only accelerate. And we are seeing this develop in real time with all suppliers of digital design tools as they integrate generative design, AI, and real-time analyses into their software suites. Firms that operate in all modes will be able to leverage auto-mated capabilities to push the design envelop and realize efficien-cies in R&D. And yes, automation will affect employment among engineers and technical specialists. The next step in this forecasted mode is the solutions themselves designing and enhancing their ca-pabilities with no human input. In a recent issue of *MIT Technology Review*, the chip maker Nvidia's efforts at using AI for autonomous driving technology is discussed. Their system uses deep learning, which has been extremely powerful at solving problems from secu-rity issues to analytics. In the case of self-driving, the software is learning so quickly that the engineers do not have a clear under-standing of how it works or of how the algorithms and routines are constructed. In terms of the Six Factors, new approaches to organi-zational design, resource management, and task allocation will be needed. How will a group of AIs in charge of design be managed and held accountable?

Another consideration is the adoption of new technology beyond digital design and collaboration tools to enhance mode develop-ment and operation. A prime example is blockchain.[1] This encryp-tion technology could have a real operational impact on managing data, design files, and knowledge within the community mode. Likewise, having secure coordination of complex designs and asso-ciated documentation among distributed members in your network mode innovation ecosystem may be invaluable. This could help al-leviate some of the issues we discussed in the case of the 787. At the same time, blockchain – as with any new technology – comes with a whole new set of questions, such as what is the right balance between data transparency and user-friendliness? How will this technology impact the human focus of design?

The answers to these questions are beyond the scope of this book, but they are important, and multimode organizations need to be prepared for these new technologies, potential new modes, and other factors we cannot foresee. But one has to learn to walk before one can run. Thus, learning to navigate the modes that the current landscape offers is an appropriate starting point. It has been our experience in executive education that we are just beginning to fill the knowledge gap that exists regarding the non-traditional innovation modes (i.e., how to approach the community mode, how to develop internal competencies to take advantage of the venture mode, etc.). And innovation is a little bit like sailing: it certainly helps to know the concepts and theories, but that alone does not make a good sailor. Therefore, becoming a multimode champion also requires practice and patience. Just as a muscle needs to be exercised to grow stronger, innovation needs to be practiced. We hope that our frameworks and tools can provide guidance for navigating this practice in the new world of innovation. Go forth and explore!

Notes

Introduction

1 Hirotaka Takeuchi and Ikujiro Nonaka, "The New New Product Development Game," *Harvard Business Review* 64 (January 1986): 321.
2 Booz, Allen, and Hamilton, Inc., *Management of New Products* (Chicago, IL: Booz, Allen, and Hamilton, Inc., 1968), 11–12.
3 Stephen K. Markham and Hyunjung Lee, "Product Development and Management Association's 2012 Comparative Performance Assessment Study," *Journal of Product Innovation Management* 30, no. 3 (May 2013): 408–29, http://onlinelibrary .wiley.com/doi/10.1111/jpim.12025/abstract.

Chapter 1

1 Alfred D. Chandler, *Strategy and Structure: Chapters in the History of the American Enterprise* (Cambridge, MA: MIT Press, 1962).
2 Frederick W. Taylor, *The Principles of Scientific Management* (New York: Harper & Brothers, 1911).
3 See, for example, Chandler, *Strategy and Structure*.
4 Kim B. Clark and Takahiro Fujimoto, *Product Development Performance* (Boston, MA: Harvard Business School Press, 1991);

Robert G. Cooper, "3rd-Generation New Product Processes," *Journal of Product Innovation Management* 11, no. 1 (1994): 3–14; Preston G. Smith and Donald G. Reinertsen, *Developing Products in Half the Time: New Rules, New Tools*, 2nd ed. (New York: Van Nostrand Reinhold, 1998).

Chapter 2

1 The exact meaning of the term "design" has been debated across various disciplines for a long time. For some, it narrowly describes the activities of specialized disciplines such as industrial design, graphic design, engineering design, or user interaction design. For others, it encompasses almost anything that is intentionally created by human beings (cf. H.A. Simon, "The Architecture of Complexity," *Proceedings of the American Philosophical Society* 106 (1962): 467–82). We use the term "digital design" here to describe the digitization of innovative activities that include both inventing and making new products, services, and solutions.

2 William D. Nordhaus, "Two Centuries of Productivity Growth in Computing," *Journal of Economic History* 67, no. 1 (March 2007): 128–59.

3 Sebastian K. Fixson and Tucker J. Marion, "Back-loading: A Potential Side Effect of Employing Digital Design Tools in New Product Development," *Journal of Product Innovation Management* 29, no. S1 (2012): 140–56.

4 Hod Lipson and Melba Kurman, *Fabricated: The New World of 3D Printing* (Indianapolis, IN: John Wiley & Sons, 2013); Chris Anderson, *Makers: The New Industrial Revolution* (New York: Crown Business, 2012).

5 Neil Howe and William Strauss, "The Next 20 Years: How Customer and Workforce Attitudes Will Evolve," *Harvard Business Review* (June–July 2007): 40–52.

6 "Internet/Broadband Fact Sheet," Pew Resource Center, last modified February 5, 2018, http://www.pewinternet.org/fact-sheet/internet-broadband/.

7 "Millennials: Coming of Age," Goldman Sachs, http://www
   .goldmansachs.com/our-thinking/pages/millennials/, accessed
   May 14, 2017.
8 Steven D. Eppinger and Anil R. Chitkara, "The New Practice
   of Global Product Development," *MIT Sloan Management
   Review* 47, no. 4 (2006): 22–30.

Chapter 3

1 Tucker J. Marion, Sebastian K. Fixson, and Marc H. Meyer,
   "The Problem with Digital Design," *Sloan Management Review*
   53, no. 4 (2012): 63–8.
2 Tucker J. Marion, Mike Reid, Erik-Jan Hultink, and Gloria
   Barczak, "The Influence of Collaborative IT Tools on NPD:
   High-performing NPD Teams Tend to Use Collaborative Tools
   Such as Wikis and Microblogs throughout the NPD Process,"
   Research-Technology Management 59, no. 2 (2016): 47–54.
3 Tucker J. Marion and John H. Friar, "Managing Global
   Outsourcing to Enhance Lean Innovation," *Research-Technology
   Management* 55, no. 5 (2012): 44–50.
4 Tucker J. Marion and Sebastian K. Fixson, "Factors Affecting
   the Use of Outside, Intermittent Resources during NPD,"
   International Journal of Innovation Science 6, no. 1 (2014): 1–18.
5 Sebastian K. Fixson and Tucker J. Marion, "When Innovation
   Stumbles: Limits to Open Innovation?" (conference proceeding,
   International Product Development Management Conference,
   Glasgow, Scotland, June 12–14, 2016).
6 Joshua Brustein, "Why GE Sees Big Things in Quirky's Little
   Inventions," *Bloomberg*, November 13, 2013, https://www
   .bloomberg.com/news/articles/2013-11-13/why-ge-sees-big
   -things-in-quirkys-little-inventions.
7 In 2017, Quirky re-emerged in its second iteration, albeit with
   a changed business model. The product portfolio is much
   smaller than with Quirky 1.0, and Quirky has left the business of manufacturing products; instead it focuses on generating ideas and concepts for established firms.

8 The degree to which a solution's architecture – be it a product, service, or system – is under the control of the focal firm may vary, but it has been theoretically argued that "designers see and seek value" (C.Y. Baldwin, "Where Do Transactions Come From? Modularity, Transactions, and the Boundaries of Firms," *Industrial and Corporate Change* 17, no. 1 (2008): 155–95), and empirically shown how industry-altering the effect can be (Sebastian K. Fixson and Jin-Kyu Park, "The Power of Integrality: Linkages between Product Architecture, Innovation, and Industry Structure," *Research Policy* 37 (2008): 1296–316).
9 "GE Garages," GE, http://www.ge.com/garages, accessed May 11, 2018.

Chapter 4

1 "GE Brilliant Factory," GE, http://www.ge.com/stories /advanced-manufacturing, accessed May 11, 2018.
2 Ted Mann and Eyk Henning, "GE Doubles Down on 3-D Printing with European Deals," *Wall Street Journal*, September 6, 2016, http://www.wsj.com/articles/ge-pays-1-4-billion-for -european-3-d-printing-firms-1473146906.
3 Interview with former GE executive (name withheld for confidentiality), November 2017.
4 David Rotman, "The 3-D Printer That Could Finally Change Manufacturing," *MIT Technology Review* 120, no. 3 (2017): 44–52.
5 Corey Clarke, "CES 2017: The 3D Printed Car Is Here," *3D Printing Industry*, January 9, 2017, https://3dprintingindustry .com/news/ces-2017-3d-printed-car-102502/.
6 Tucker J. Marion, Mike Reid, Erik-Jan Hultink, and Gloria Barczak, "The Influence of Collaborative IT Tools on NPD: High-performing NPD Teams Tend to Use Collaborative Tools Such as Wikis and Microblogs throughout the NPD Process," *Research-Technology Management* 59, no. 2 (2016): 47–54.
7 Yang Zhao, "Your Business Isn't Really 'Multinational,'" *Huffington Post*, October 3, 2016, http://www.huffingtonpost

.com/entry/your-business-isnt-really-multinational_us_57e29d
f5e4b05d3737be5243.

8 "Case Study: SpaceX Delivers Outer Space at Bargain Rates,"
Siemens PLM Software, https://www.plm.automation.siemens
.com/en/about_us/success/case_study.cfm?component=30328
&ComponentTemplate=1481, accessed May 11, 2018.

9 Bridget Butler O'Neal, "Ready for Blast Off? SpaceX 3D Printed
SuperDraco Thrusters Prove Themselves Further at Texas Rocket
Facility," 3DPrint.com, November 13, 2015, https://3dprint
.com/105511/spacex-3d-printed-superdraco/.

10 Sarah Miller Caldicott, "Why Ford's Alan Mulally Is an Innovation CEO for the Record Books," *Forbes*, June 25, 2014, http://
www.forbes.com/sites/sarahcaldicott/2014/06/25/why-fords
-alan-mulally-is-an-innovation-ceo-for-the-record-books/.

11 Don Reisinger, "Samsung Wins Appeal in $120M Patent Fight
with Apple," *Fortune*, February 26, 2016, http://fortune.com
/2016/02/26/apple-samsung-patent-appeal/.

12 Tucker J. Marion, Denise Dunlap, and John Friar, "Instilling the
Entrepreneurial Spirit in Your R&D Team: What Large Firms
Can Learn from Successful Start-ups," *IEEE Transactions on
Engineering Management* 59, no. 2 (2012): 323–37.

13 Marc H. Meyer and Tucker J. Marion, "Innovating for
Effectiveness: Lessons from Design Firms," *Research-Technology
Management* 5 (2010): 21–8.

14 Stan Phelps, "Cracking Into Google: 15 Reasons Why More
Than 2 Million People Apply Each Year," *Forbes*, August 5, 2014,
http://www.forbes.com/sites/stanphelps/2014/08/05
/cracking-into-google-the-15-reasons-why-over-2-million
-people-apply-each-year/.

15 Brandon Turkus, "Elon Musk Says Apple Offering $250,000
Signing Bonus to Poach Tesla Employees," *Autoblog*, February 7,
2015, http://www.autoblog.com/2015/02/07/elon-musk
-apple-hiring-tesla-workers/.

16 "Proceedings of ICED 09, the 17th International Conference
on Engineering Design, Vol. 3, Design Organization and
Management, Palo Alto, CA, USA, 24–27.08.2009," *The Design*

Society, https://www.designsociety.org/publication/28507
/ds_58-3_proceedings_of_iced_09_the_17th_international
_conference_on_engineering_design_vol_3_design_organi
zation_and_management_palo_alto_ca_usa_24-27_08_2009.

17 Marc H. Meyer and Tucker J. Marion, "Preserving the Integrity
of Knowledge and Information in R&D," *Business Horizons* 56,
no. 1 (2013): 51–61.

18 Denise Dunlap, Ronaldo Parente, Jose-Mauricio Geleilate, and
Tucker J. Marion, "Organizing for Innovation Ambidexterity in
Emerging Markets Taking Advantage of Supplier Involvement
and Foreignness," *Journal of Leadership & Organizational Studies*
23, no. 2 (March 2016): 175–90.

19 Chuck Squatriglia, "Bob Lutz: Volt Is U.S. Car Industry's Moon
Shot," *Wired*, January 15, 2008, https://www.wired.com
/2008/01/bob-lutz-volt-is-u-s-car-industrys-moon-shot/.

20 Larry Edsall, *Chevrolet Volt: Charging into the Future*
(Minneapolis, MN: Motorbooks, 2010).

Chapter 5

1 Chaitanya Ramalingegowda, "[Famous Failures] The Grocery
E-tailer That Raised Over $800 Million and Went Public Before
Filing for Bankruptcy," *YourStory*, September 15, 2014, https://
yourstory.com/2014/09/webvan-e-tailer/.

2 Eric Ries, *The Lean Startup* (New York: Crown Business, 2011);
Steve Blank, "Why the Lean Start-up Changes Everything,"
Harvard Business Review (May 2013), https://hbr.org/2013/05
/why-the-lean-start-up-changes-everything.

3 InVision: The Digital Product Design Platform Powering the
World's Best User Experiences, www.invisionapp.com.

4 Tucker J. Marion, Kim A. Eddleston, John H. Friar, and David
Deeds, "The Evolution of Interorganizational Relationships in
Emerging Ventures: An Ethnographic Study within the New
Product Development Process," *Journal of Business Venturing* 30,
no. 1 (2015): 167–84.

5 "MassChallenge Boston," MassChallenge, http://boston
   .masschallenge.org/, accessed May 14, 2018.
6 "What We Do," IDEA, http://www.northeastern.edu/idea/,
   accessed May 14, 2018.
7 "Dorm Room Fund," Dorm Room Fund, http://dormroom
   fund.com/, accessed May 14, 2018.
8 Calvin Smith, Sebastian K. Fixson, Carlos Paniagua-Ferrari,
   and Salvatore Parise, "Evolution of an Innovation Capability:
   Making Crowdsourcing Work within a Large Enterprise,"
   Research-Technology Management 60, no. 2 (2017): 26–35.
9 "First Build," First Build, https://firstbuild.com/, accessed
   May 14, 2018.
10 "Opal Nugget Ice Maker," Indiegogo, last modified August 27,
   2015, https://www.indiegogo.com/projects/opal-nugget
   -ice-maker/.
11 Tucker J. Marion, John H. Friar, and Timothy W. Simpson,
   "New Product Development Practices and Early-Stage Firms:
   Two In-Depth Case Studies," *Journal of Product Innovation
   Management* 29, no. 4 (2012): 639–54; Marion, Dunlap,
   and Friar, "Instilling the Entrepreneurial Spirit in Your
   R&D Team."
12 Tucker Marion, Denise Dunlap, and John Friar, "Instilling the
   Entrepreneurial Spirit in Your R&D Team: What Large Firms
   Can Learn from Successful Start-ups," *IEEE Transactions on
   Engineering Management* 59, no. 2 (2012): 323–37.
13 Ibid.
14 From a research interview published online at the *Innovation
   Leader*, with Tucker J. Marion, 2015, https://www.innovation
   leader.com/qa-ten-elements-of-lean-innovation/.
15 Kyle Vanhemert, "Look Inside Apple's Spaceship Headquarters
   with 24 All-New Renderings," *Wired*, November 11, 2013,
   https://www.wired.com/2013/11/a-glimpse-into-apples
   -crazy-new-spaceship-headquarters/.
16 See the work by Amy C. Edmondson, e.g., "Psychological
   Safety and Learning Behavior in Work Teams," *Administrative*

Science Quarterly 44, no. 2 (1999): 350–83; and *Teaming: How Organizations Learn, Innovate, and Compete in the Knowledge Economy* (San Francisco: John Wiley and Sons, 2012).

17 Clifton B. Parker, "Japan Transforming Its Innovation Culture by Changing Social Norms, Stanford Scholar Finds," *Stanford News*, August 31, 2016, http://news.stanford.edu/2016/08/31/japan-transforming-innovation-culture/.

18 "About," IDEA, http://www.northeastern.edu/idea/about/, accessed May 11, 2018.

19 "How Constant Contact Blends Lean Startup & Design Thinking," Innovation Leader, https://www.innovationleader.com/how-constant-contact-blends-lean-startup-and-design-thinking/, accessed May 23, 2018. See also the Constant Contact InnoLoft. See also "Meet the 3 Teams Driving Internal Innovation at Citrix," Medium, https://medium.com/@innovatorspro/meet-the-3-teams-driving-internal-innovation-at-citrix-94c13f275203, accessed May 23, 2018.

20 Marion, Dunlap, and Friar, "Instilling the Entrepreneurial Spirit in Your R&D Team."

21 Tucker Marion, Sebastian Fixson, and Marc H. Meyer, "The Problem with Digital Design," *MIT Sloan Management Review* 53, no. 4 (2012): 63.

Chapter 6

1 "GrabCAD," Wikipedia, https://en.wikipedia.org/wiki/GrabCAD, accessed November 6, 2016.

2 Ingrid Lunden, "3D Printing Company Stratasys Is Buying GrabCAD for Around $100M, Beating Out Autodesk, Adobe," *Tech Crunch*, September 16, 2014, https://techcrunch.com/2014/09/16/3d-printing-company-stratasys-is-buying-grabcad-for-around-100m/.

3 Henry W. Chesbrough, *Open Innovation: The New Imperative for Creating and Profiting from Technology* (Boston, MA: Harvard Business Press, 2003).

4 Attributed to Sun Microsystem's co-founder Bill Joy; see
   K.R. Lakhani and J.A. Panetta, "The Principles of Distributed
   Innovation," *Innovations* 2, no. 3 (2007): 97–112.
5 "Congratulations to Our Winners!" XPRIZE, http://tricorder
   .xprize.org/teams, accessed November 16, 2016.
6 "Our Solvers," InnoCentive, https://www.innocentive.com
   /our-solvers/, accessed November 8, 2016.
7 Yet2 is another innovation intermediary: http://www.yet2
   .com/, accessed November 8, 2016.
8 This page has since been taken down from NineSigma's website,
   but a snapshot of the solution provider survey infographic can
   still be seen via the WayBack Machine: "Infographic: NineSigma
   Solution Provider Survey," WayBack Machine, August 20, 2016,
   https://web.archive.org/web/20160820082807/http://nine
   sigma.com/infographic-ninesigma-solution-provider-survey
   /ninesigma-sp-survey-infographic.
9 "Open Innovation," Unilever, https://www.unilever.com
   /about/innovation/open-innovation/, accessed May 11, 2018.
10 Tucker J. Marion, Gloria Barczak, and Erik-Jan Hultink,
   "Do Social Media Tools Impact the Development Phase? An
   Exploratory Study," *Journal of Product Innovation Management* 31,
   no. S1 (2014): 18–29.
11 "Open Technology: Building for Future Innovation," IBM,
   http://www.ibm.com/it-infrastructure/us-en/open
   -innovation/, accessed November 16, 2016.
12 Panel discussion transcript from Tim Thomas, former CIO
   of Local Motors. "Collaborating with External Partners"
   with Ludwig Bstieler, David Lazer, and Tim Thomas at
   the Collaborative Innovation Networks Conference, May
   2013. Theconference is sponsored by the Institute for Global
   Innovation Management and the D'Amore-McKim School of
   Business, Northeastern University, Boston, MA. https://www
   .youtube.com/watch?v=INt9eqB1sLI.
13 Mikotaj Jan Piskorski, "Social Strategies That Work," *Harvard
   Business Review*, November 2011, https://hbr.org/2011/11
   /social-strategies-that-work; Tucker J. Marion, Deborah Roberts,

Marina Candi and Gloria Barczak, "Customizing Your Social Strategy to the Platform," *MIT Sloan Management Review*, March 30, 2016, http://sloanreview.mit.edu/article /customizing-your-social-strategy-to-the-platform/; Marina Candi, Deborah Roberts, Tucker Marion and Gloria Barczak, "Social Strategy to Gain Knowledge for Innovation," *British Journal of Management* (December 2017), DOI: 10.1111/1467 -8551.12280.

14 "Collaborating with External Partners," Collaborative Innovation Networks Conference.

15 "Open Innovation Initiative: General Conditions," Airbus Helicopters, last modified June 2016, http://www.helicopters .airbus.com/website/docs_wsw/RUB_348/tile_3379/General _conditions_Open_Innovation_AH_2016.pdf.

16 David Antons and Frank T. Piller, "Opening the Black Box of 'Not Invented Here': Attitudes, Decision Biases, and Behavioral Consequences," *Academy of Management Perspectives* 29, no. 2 (2015): 193–217.

17 Karim R. Lakhani, Hila Lifschitz-Assaf, and Michael L. Tushman, "Open Innovation and Organizational Boundaries: Task Decomposition, Knowledge Distribution and the Locus of Innovation," in *Handbook of Economic Organization*, ed. Anna Grandori (Cheltenham, UK: Edward Elgar, 2013), 355–82.

18 "PTC ThingWorx Joins MK: Smart to Enable Rapid Development for Internet of Things Applications," PTC, February 10, 2016, http://www.ptc.com/news/2016/ptc -thingworx-joins-mk-smart.

19 "HYVE Crowd: Solving the Unsolvable," HYVE Crowd, https://www.hyvecrowd.com/start, accessed May 14, 2018.

20 Raffaella Manzini, Valentina Lazzarotti, and Luisa Pellegrini, "How to Remain as Closed as Possible in the Open Innovation Era: The Case of Lindt & Sprüngli," *Long Range Planning* 50, no. 2 (2017): 260–81.

21 Interview/discussion in March 2015, Seattle, WA.

22 D'Amore-McKim School of Business, "Tim Thomas' Presentation at the Collaborative Innovation Networks Conference,"

Northeastern University, May 31, 2013, https://www.youtube
.com/watch?v=h36-b7sULig.

Chapter 7

1 Sy Mukherjee, "Prepare for the Digital Health Revolution,"
  Fortune Magazine, April 20, 2017, http://fortune.com
  /2017/04/20/digital-health-revolution/.
2 Tucker J. Marion, Henri J. Thevenot, and Timothy W. Simpson,
  "A Cost-based Methodology for Evaluating Product Platform
  Commonality Sourcing Decisions with Two Examples,"
  International Journal of Production Research 45, no. 22 (2007):
  5285–308.
3 Peter Coy, "Just How Cheap Is Chinese Labor," *Business Week
  Online*, December 13, 2004, https://www.bloomberg.com
  /news/articles/2004-12-12/just-how-cheap-is-chinese-labor.
4 Tucker J. Marion, Henri J. Thevenot, and Timothy W. Simpson,
  "A Cost-based Methodology for Evaluating Product Platform
  Commonality Sourcing Decisions with Two Examples,"
  International Journal of Production Research 45, no. 22 (2007):
  5285–308.
5 Field research performed at Pennsylvania State University from
  2006 to 2007. Manufacturing locus investigation of retail stores
  such as Target performed for a graduate school project.
6 Mike Colias, "Americans Embrace a Made-in-China Buick SUV,"
  Wall Street Journal, October 6, 2016, http://www.wsj.com
  /articles/americans-embrace-a-made-in-china-buick-suv
  -1475771438.
7 Charles Duhigg and Keith Bradsher, "Apple's Jobs to Obama:
  'Jobs Aren't Coming Back' to US," *Herald-Tribune*, January23,
  2012, http://www.heraldtribune.com/news/20120123
  /apples-jobs-to-obama-jobs-arent-coming-back-to-us; Duhigg
  and Bradsher, "How the US Lost Out on iPhone Work,"
  New York Times, January 21, 2012, http://www.nytimes.com
  /2012/01/22/business/apple-america-and-a-squeezed-middle
  -class.html.

8 Matt Brian, "Steve Jobs-Designed Apple Factory, the Birthplace of the Macintosh, Considered Historic Status," *The Next Web,* October 2, 2012, http://thenextweb.com/apple/2012/10/02 /steve-jobs-designed-apple-factory-the-birthplace-of-the -macintosh-considered-for-historic-status/.

9 Adam Fisher, "Payback Time," *Wired Magazine,* November 2017, 108.

10 Steven Levy, "The Perfect Thing," *Wired Magazine,* November 2006, 136, https://www.wired.com/2006/11/ipod/.

11 Charles Duhigg and Keith Bradsher, "How the U.S. Lost Out on iPhone Work," *New York Times,* January 21, 2012, https:// www.nytimes.com/2012/01/22/business/apple-america-and -a-squeezed-middle-class.html.

12 "Mac Pro," Apple, http://www.apple.com/mac-pro/, accessed May 14, 2018.

13 Kyle Wiggers, "Could Apple's Next iPhones Be Made in the USA," Yahoo, January 23, 2017, https://finance.yahoo.com /news/trump-effect-apple-may-consider-184924422.html.

14 Gloria Barczak, Abbie Griffin, and Ken B. Kahn, "Trends and Drivers of Success in NPD Practices: Results of the 2003 PDMA Best Practices Study," *Journal of Product Innovation Management* 26, no. 1 (2009): 3–23.

15 Steve Denning, "What Went Wrong at Boeing?" *Forbes,* January 21, 2013, http://www.forbes.com/sites/stevedenning /2013/01/21/what-went-wrong-at-boeing/.

16 Nicola Clark, "The Airbus Saga: Crossed Wires and a Multibillion-Euro Delay," *New York Times,* December 11, 2006, http://www.nytimes.com/2006/12/11/business/world business/11iht-airbus.3860198.html.

17 Tucker J. Marion, Sebastian K. Fixson, and Marc H. Meyer, "The Problem with Digital Design," *MIT Sloan Management Review* 53, no. 4 (2012): 63–8.

18 Timothy Kayworth and Dorothy Leidner, "The Global Virtual Manager: A Prescription for Success," *European Management Journal* 18, no. 2 (2000): 183–94.

19 Tucker J. Marion and Sebastian K. Fixson, "Factors Affecting the Use of Outside, Intermittent Resources During

NPD," *International Journal of Innovation Science* 6, no. 1 (2014): 1–18.

20 Ibid.

21 Ibid.

22 Ibid.

23 Adam Lashinsky, *Inside Apple: How America's Most Admired – and Secretive – Company Really Works* (New York: Business Plus, 2012).

24 Fred Lambert, "A Number of Companies Are Now Using Tesla's Open-source Patents and It Has Some Interesting Implications," Electrek, November 10, 2015, https://electrek .co/2015/11/10/a-number-of-companies-are-now-using -teslas-open-source-patents-and-it-has-some-interesting -implications/.

25 Marion and Fixson, "Factors Affecting the Use of Outside, Intermittent Resources."

26 David Greising and Julie Johnsson, "Behind Boeing's 787 Delays," *Chicago Tribune*, December 8, 2007, http://articles .chicagotribune.com/2007-12-08/news/0712070870_1_dream liner-boeing-spokeswoman-suppliers.

27 L.J. Hart-Smith, "Out-sourced Profits: The Cornerstone of Successful Subcontracting" (symposium presentation at the Boeing Third Annual Technical Excellence Symposium in St. Louis, MO, February 14–15, 2001), http://seattletimes .nwsource.com/ABPub/2011/02/04/2014130646.pdf.

28 John W. Henke Jr. and Chun Zhang, "Increasing Supplier-Driven Innovation," *MIT Sloan Management Review* 51, no. 2 (2010), https://sloanreview.mit.edu/article/increasing -supplier-driven-innovation/.

29 Tucker J. Marion, Kim A. Eddleston, John H. Friar, and David Deeds, "The Evolution of Interorganizational Relationships in Emerging Ventures: An Ethnographic Study within the New Product Development Process," *Journal of Business Venturing* 30, no. 1 (2015): 167–84.

30 PaperPro (Accentra, Inc.) was acquired by Amax, Inc., in 2012. The research described here was undertaken from 2005 to 2007.

31 Tucker J. Marion, "New Product Development in Early-Stage Firms" (PhD diss., Pennsylvania State University, 2007).

32 Ibid.

33 Ibid.

34 Tucker J. Marion and Timothy W. Simpson, "New Product Development Practice Application to an Early-Stage Firm: The Case of the PaperPro® StackMaster™," *Design Studies* 30, no. 5 (2009): 561–87.

35 Henke and Zhang, "Increasing Supplier-Driven Innovation."

36 Arthur St. Antoine, "John Deere 1050K: The Ultimate Building Machine," *Automobile Magazine*, November 27, 2017, http://www.automobilemag.com/news/john-deere-1050k-ultimate-building-machine/.

37 Paul Nunes and Larry Downes, "At Haier and Lenovo, Chinese-Style Open Innovation," *Forbes*, September 26, 2016, https://www.forbes.com/sites/bigbangdisruption/2016/09/26/at-haier-and-lenovo-chinese-style-open-innovation/.

38 Marion et al., "The Evolution of Interorganizational Relationships in Emerging Ventures."

39 Tucker J. Marion and John H. Friar, "Managing Global Outsourcing to Enhance Lean Innovation," *Research-Technology Management* 55, no. 5 (2012): 44–50.

40 Tucker J. Marion, "4 Factors That Predict Startup Success, and One That Doesn't," *Harvard Business Review*, May 3, 2016, https://hbr.org/2016/05/4-factors-that-predict-startup-success-and-one-that-doesnt.

41 James Fallows, "How America Is Putting Itself Back Together," *Atlantic*, March 2016, http://www.theatlantic.com/magazine/archive/2016/03/how-america-is-putting-itself-back-together/426882/.

42 Tucker J. Marion, Denise R. Dunlap, and John H. Friar, "The University Entrepreneur: A Census and Survey of Attributes and Outcomes," *R&D Management* 42, no. 5 (2012): 401–19.

43 Marion et al., "Evolution of Interorganizational Relationships in Emerging Ventures."

44 V.G. Narayanan and Ananth Raman, "Aligning Incentives in Supply Chains," *Harvard Business Review*, November 2004, https://hbr.org/2004/11/aligning-incentives-in-supply -chains.
45 Katsuki Aoki and Thomas Taro Lennerfors, "The New Improved Keiretsu," *Harvard Business Review*, September 2013, https:// hbr.org/2013/09/the-new-improved-keiretsu.

Chapter 8

1 Bharat Kapoor, Kevin Nolan, and Natarajan Venkatakrishnan, "How GE Applicances Built an Innovation Lab to Rapidly Prototype Products," *Harvard Business Review*, July 21, 2017, https://hbr.org/2017/07/how-ge-built-an-innovation-lab-to -rapidly-prototype-appliances.
2 George Castellion and Stephen K. Markham, "Perspective: New Product Failure Rates: Influence of *Argumentum Ad Populum* and Self-interest," *Journal of Product Innovation Management* 30, no. 5 (2013): 976–9.
3 Michael Marks, David Hoyt, "Quirky: A Business Based on Making Invention Accessible," Stanford Business, 2013, https:// www.gsb.stanford.edu/faculty-research/case-studies /quirky-business-based-making-invention-accessible.
4 Autodesk, "Hot-Rodders Pioneer a New Manufacturing Revolution," https://www.autodesk.com/customer-stories /hack-rod, accessed May 14, 2018.
5 John Rosevear, "Why Ford and General Motors Teamed Up on Transmissions," *Fool*, May 22, 2016, https://www.fool.com /investing/general/2016/05/22/why-ford-and-general-motors -teamed-up-on-transmiss.aspx.
6 "GM to Open IT Innovation Center in Georgia," *GM*, January 10, 2013, http://media.gm.com/media/us/en/gm /news.detail.html/content/Pages/news/us/en/2013/Jan /0110_atl-it-ctr.html.
7 Adam Kress, "GE and Local Motors Announce Fuse, a New Business Model for Agile Manufacturing," *Launch*

Forth, October 18, 2016, https://launchforth.io/blog/post
/ge-and-local-motors-announce-fuse/2193/.

8 Hirotaka Takeuchi and Ikujiro Nonaka, "The New New Product
Development Game," *Harvard Business Review* 64 (January
1986): 321.

Conclusion

1 Marco Iansiti and Karim R. Lakhani, "The Truth About
Blockchain," *Harvard Business Review*, January 2017, https://
hbr.org/2017/01/the-truth-about-blockchain.

Index

3D printing: "3D print" function, 19; 3D Systems, 30, 73; and ACEINNA, Inc., 55–6; as additive manufacturing technology, 17; and aircraft design, xi, 16, 21, 26–7, 51–2, 55, 58; Arcam, 51; and automotive design, 53–4; and Continuum, 56; Divergent, 53–4; easy-to-use, 80; and firm self-assessment, 67; and General Electric (GE), 51–2; Hackrod, 143; impact of, xi, 51–2; introduction of, 16; leveraging, 50, 51; and medical devices, 52–3; and minimally viable products (MVPs), 69, 73, 77, 82; low-cost, 17, 20, 21; new applications for, 27–8; and PaperPro, 121, 122; service providers, 30; SLM Solutions, 51; Stratasys, 19–20, 87; and start-ups, 30, 53, 72, 73

3D Systems, 30, 73

100kgarages.com, 30, 73

ACEINNA, Inc., 55–6

additive manufacturing. *See* 3D printing

Airbus: and 3D printing, 27; A380, 116; and the community mode, 91, 133; Helicopters and intellectual property (IP), 92; and Local Motors, 91, 146; as a multimode organization, 133, 146; and the network mode, 114

aircraft design: and 3D printing, xi, 16, 21, 26–7, 51–2, 58; and ACEINNA, Inc., 55; and computer-aided design (CAD), 6, 16, 58. *See also* Airbus; Boeing 787; SpaceX